NO ONE LEFT TO LIE TO

V

NO ONE LEFT TO LIE TO

THE TRIANGULATIONS OF WILLIAM JEFFERSON CLINTON

CHRISTOPHER HITCHENS

VERSO

London • New York

First published by Verso 1999
Paperback edition first published by Verso 2000

VERSO

UK: 6 Meard Street, London W1V 3HR
USA: 180 Varick Street, New York, NY 10014-4606

Verso is the imprint of New Left Books

ISBN 1-85984-284-4

British Library Cataloguing in Publication Data
A catalogue record for this book is available from the British Library

Library of Congress Cataloging-in-Publication Data
A catalog record for this book is available from the Library of Congress

Printed by R.R. Donnelley & Sons, USA

CONTENTS

They were careless people, Tom and Daisy—they smashed up things and creatures and then retreated back into their money or their vast carelessness, or whatever it was that kept them together, and let other people clean up the mess they had made . . .

—F. Scott Fitzgerald, *The Great Gatsby*

ACKNOWLEDGMENTS

THANKS ARE DUE to all those on the Left who saw the menace of Clinton, and who resisted the moral and political blackmail which silenced and shamed the liberal herd. In particular, I should like to thank Perry Anderson, Marc Cooper, Patrick Caddell, Doug Ireland, Bruce Shapiro, Barbara Ehrenreich, Gwendolyn Mink, Sam Husseini (for his especial help on the health-care racket), Robin Blackburn, Roger Morris, Joseph Heller, and Jamin Raskin. Many honorable conservative friends also deserve my thanks, for repudiating Clintonism even when it served their immediate and (I would say) exorbitant political needs. They might prefer not to be thanked by name.

The experience of beginning such an essay in a state of relative composure, and then finishing it amid the collapsing scenery of a show-trial and an unfolding scandal of multinational proportions—only hinted at here—was a vertiginous one. I could not have attempted it or undergone it without Carol Blue, whose instinct for justice and whose contempt for falsity has been my loving insurance for a decade.

Christopher Hitchens
Washington, D.C., March 1999

For Laura Antonia and Sophia Mando,
my daughters

PREFACE

THIS LITTLE BOOK has no "hidden agenda." It is offered in the most cheerful and open polemical spirit, as an attack on a crooked president and a corrupt and reactionary administration. Necessarily, it also engages with the stratagems that have been employed to shield that president and that administration. And it maintains, even insists, that the two most salient elements of Clintonism—the personal crookery on the one hand, and the cowardice and conservatism on the other—are indissolubly related. I have found it frankly astonishing and sometimes alarming, not just since January of 1998 but since January of 1992, to encounter the dust storm of bogus arguments that face anyone prepared to make such a simple case. A brief explanation—by no means to be mistaken for an apologia—may be helpful.

Some years ago, I was approached, as were my editors at *Vanity Fair*, by a woman claiming to be the mother of a child by Clinton. (I decline to use the word "illegitimate" as a description of a baby, and may as well say at once that this is not my only difference with the supposedly moral majority, or indeed with any other congregation or—the *mot juste*—"flock.") The woman seemed superficially convincing; the attached photographs had an almost offputting resemblance to the putative father; the child was—if only by the rightly discredited test of *Plessy v. Ferguson*—black. The mother had, at the time of his conception, been reduced to selling her body for money. We had a little editorial conference about it. Did Hitchens want to go to Australia, where the woman then was? Well, Hitchens had always wanted to go to Australia. But here are the reasons why I turned down such a tempting increment on my frequent-flyer mileage program.

First of all—and even assuming the truth of the story—the little boy had been conceived when Mr. Clinton was the governor of Arkansas. At that time, the bold governor had not begun his highly popular campaign against defenseless indigent mothers. Nor had he emerged as the upright scourge of the "deadbeat dad" or absent father. The woman—perhaps because she had African genes and worked as a prostitute—had not been rewarded with a state job, even of the lowly kind bestowed on Gennifer Flowers. There seemed, in other words, to be no political irony or contradiction of the sort that sometimes licenses a righteous press in the exposure of iniquity. There was, further, the question of Mrs. and Miss Clinton. If Hillary Clinton, hardened as she doubtless was (I would now say, as she undoubtedly *is*), was going to find that she had a sudden step-daughter, that might perhaps be one thing. But Chelsea Clinton was then aged about twelve. An unexpected black half-brother (quite close to her own age) might have been just the right surprise for her. On the other hand, it might not. I didn't feel it was my job to decide this. My friends Graydon Carter and Elise O'Shaughnessy, I'm pleased to say, were in complete agreement. A great story in one way: but also a story we would always have regretted breaking. Even when I *did* go to Australia for the magazine, some time later, I took care to leave the woman's accusing dossier behind.

Like a number of other people in Washington, I had heard a third-hand version of her tale during the election of 1992. In the briefly famous documentary *The War Room*, which hymns the spinning skills of thugs like James Carville, George Stephanopoulos can be seen "live" on the telephone, deftly fending off a nutcase Ross Perot supporter who has called in about the "bastard." The caller may not have said "black bastard," but one didn't have to be unduly tender-minded to notice that Clinton—however much he had tried to charm and woo them—still had enemies on the Right. Some of these enemies had allowed themselves to become infected, or were infected already, with the filthy taint of racism. That seemed an additional reason for maintaining a certain . . . reserve. I wasn't to know that, by the middle of 1998, Clinton's hacks would be using the bigotry of some of his critics, in the same way that Johnnie Cochrane had employed the sick racist cop Mark Fuhrman, to change the subject and to "whiten" the sepulcher.

Just as the Republican case against the president seemed to be lapsing into incoherence, in the first days of 1999, Matt Drudge uncorked the black baby again. Indeed, he curtain-raised this nonexclusive at the annual gathering of the cultural and political Right, held in San Diego as a rival attraction to the pulverizing tedium and self-regard of the Clintonian "Renaissance Weekend" at Hilton Head. Once put to the most perfunctory forensic test, the whole story collapsed within the space of twenty-four hours. Mr. Clinton's DNA—famously found dabbled on the costly Gap garment of a credulous intern—was sufficiently knowable from the indices of the Starr Report for a preliminary finding to be possible. There was nothing like a "match" between the two genetic attributes. Once again, and for reasons of professional rather than political feeling, I felt glad that Graydon Carter and I had put privacy (and scruples that arose partly from the fatherhood of our own daughters) ahead of sensation all those years ago.

Still, I couldn't but notice that White House spokesmen, when bluntly asked about the Drudge story by reporters, reacted as if it *could* be true. There was nothing about their Leader, they seemed to convey by the etiolated remains of their body language, that might not one day need a "privacy" defense, however hastily or wildly concocted. It turned out, however, that Mr. Drudge had done them another unintended favor. Nothing is more helpful, to a person with a record of economizing with the truth, than a false and malicious and disprovable allegation. And Drudge—whose want of discrimination in this respect is almost a trademark—openly says that he'll print anything and let the customers decide what's actually kosher. This form of pretended "consumer sovereignty" is fraudulent in the same way that its analogues are. (It means, for one thing, that you have no right to claim that you were correct, or truthful, or brave. All you did was pass it on, like a leaker or some other kind of conduit. The death of any intelligent or principled journalism is foreshadowed by such promiscuity.) In the old days, true enough, the Washington press corps was a megaphone for "official sources." Now, it's a megaphone for official sources *and* traders from the toilet.

Just such a symbiosis—comparable to his affectless equidistance between left and right, Republican and Democrat, white-collar crime and blue-collar crime, true and false, sacred and profane, bought and paid for, public and private, *quid* and *quo*—happened to serve Mr. Clinton well on the day in January 1998 that his presidency went into eclipse, or seemed about to do so. He made the most ample possible use of the natural reticence and decency that is felt by people who open a bedroom or bathroom door without knocking. (And this, even though he was the occupant of said bathroom and bedroom.) He also made a masterly use of the apparent contrast between the trivial and the serious. But on this occasion, and having watched it for some years, I felt confident that I could see through his shell game. On the first day, and in the presence of witnesses, I said: "This time he's going to be impeached." And, in support of my own much underrated and even mocked prescience, I will quote what the *Los Angeles Times* was kind enough to print under my name on January 28, 1998:

> Montesquieu remarked that if a great city or a great state should fall as the result of an apparent "accident," then there would be a general reason why it required only an accident to make it fall. This may appear to be a tautology, but it actually holds up very well as a means of analyzing what we lazily refer to as a "sex scandal."
>
> If a rust-free zipper were enough on its own to cripple a politician, then quite clearly Bill Clinton would be remembered, if at all, as a mediocre Governor of the great state of Arkansas. It is therefore silly to describe the present unseemly furor as a prurient outburst over one man's apparently self-destructive sexual compulsions.
>
> Until recently, this same man was fairly successfully fighting a delaying action against two long-standing complaints. The first was that he had imported unsavory Arkansas business practices to Washington, along with some of the unsavory practitioners like the disgraced

Webster Hubbell. The second was that he viewed stray women employees as spoils along the trail.

Think of these two strands as wires, neither of them especially
"live." (Everybody knew something about both, and few people
believed that there was no substance to either story, but a fairly general benefit of the doubt was still being awarded.) Now the two wires
have touched, and crossed, and crackled. Vernon Jordan's fellow
board-members at Revlon gave a suspiciously large "consultancy"
contract to Hubbell at just the moment when his usefulness as anybody's attorney had come to an end. (He was, after all, not just quit-
ting the Department of Justice but going straight to jail.) And now
this same well of Revlon is revisited by the busy Mr. Jordan when it
comes time to furnish Monica Lewinsky with a soft landing. So, does
this represent a Clinton machine *modus operandi* when it comes to
potentially embarrassing witnesses? Kenneth Starr would be failing in
his mandate as Independent Counsel if he did not put the question,
and press hard for an answer. Even more to the point, so would we.
This was all waiting to happen. . . .

Or consider Dick Morris, Clinton's other best friend. The tarts from
the "escort service" we could have—with a slight shudder—overlooked.
But Morris's carryings-on in the Jefferson Hotel were an allegory of the
way business was being conducted at the Democratic National
Committee and even in the franchising of the Lincoln Bedroom. His
exorbitant political bills necessitated the debauching, not just of himself, but of a whole presidential election. So that dirty little story served
to illuminate the dirty big story. As does this one. . . .

Had Clinton begun by saying: "Yes, I did love Gennifer, but that's
my business," many of us would have rejoiced and defended him.
Instead, he disowned and insulted her and said he'd been innocent of
that adultery, and treated the voters as if they were saps. Having
apparently put Ms. Lewinsky into the quick-fix world of Jordan and

Morris, he is in no position to claim that it's a private emotional matter, and has no right to confuse his business with that of the country's. Which is why he has a scandal on "his" hands, and is also why we need feel no pang when he falsely claims that the press and public are wasting his valuable time, when the truth is exactly the other way about.

I sat back after writing that, and sat back rather pleased with myself after reading it in print, and thought that some people would take my point even if they didn't agree with it, and then went through a year in which, not once but several times every day, I was informed that Clinton had lied only to protect his wife and daughter (and, OK, himself) from shame! In the course of that same year, his wife and daughter were exposed by Clinton to repeated shame and humiliation. Dick Morris emerged as the only person to whom Clinton told the truth. Vernon Jordan emerged as the crucial witness in a matter of obstruction of justice. "Notice how they always trash the accusers," said Erik Tarloff to me one day. Erik who has contributed to speeches for Clinton and Gore and is married to Laura D'Andrea Tyson, former chair of Clinton's Council of Economic Advisors. "They destroy their reputations. If Monica hadn't had that blue dress, they were getting ready to portray her as a fantasist and an erotomaniac. Imagine what we'd all be thinking of her now." Nor was this an exaggeration. In parallel with its Robert Rubin/Alan Greenspan presentation of bankerly orthodoxy and unshakeable respectability, the Clinton administration always had its banana republic side. For all the talk about historic presidential "philandering," it is hard to recall any other White House which has had to maintain a quasi-governmental or para-state division devoted exclusively to the bullying and defamation of women. Like my old friend, there were many who "didn't like to think about it." Even Clinton's best friend, the notably unfastidious Dick Morris, once told CNBC:

> Under Betsey Wright's supervision in the 1992 Clinton campaign, there was an entire operation funded with over $100,000 of campaign money, which included federal matching funds, to hire private detectives to go into the personal lives of women who were alleged to have had sex with Bill Clinton. To develop compromising material—blackmailing information, basically—to coerce them into signing affidavits saying they did not have sex with Bill Clinton.

"Having sex" was the most fragrant and presentable way of describing the experience of certain women, like the Arkansas nursing-home supervisor Juanita Broaddrick, who was raped by Clinton while he was state attorney general in 1978. [See Chapter Six.] Even as the 1999 impeachment trial was in progress, NBC was withholding a long interview with this extremely credible and principled lady, whose affidavit sat in the "evidence room" at the House of Representatives. No Democrat ever went to look at the evidence, and this was not because of its presumed untruth. (By then, the use of the mantra "consensual sex" had become part of consensual, or consensus, politics.) And women who told the truth were accused, at best, of trying to lure a sitting president into a "perjury trap." As if it were necessary to trick Clinton into telling a lie . . . .

Of course, in a time of "sexual McCarthyism" there's probably some advantage in being prudent. Take this little item, which appeared deadpan on page A10 of the *Washington Post* on January 30, 1999. It concerned the testimony of an "investigator" who had been hired to keep an eye on Ms. Kathleen Willey. Ms. Willey, some may recall, had been an admirer of President Clinton, had been the wife of a Democratic fund-raiser, had been a volunteer worker at the White House, had suddenly become a widow, had gone in distress to the Oval Office for comfort and for a discussion about the possibility of a paying job, and had been rewarded with a crushing embrace, some clichéd words of bar-room courtship, and the guiding by the presidential mitt of her own hand onto his distended penis. (That is, if you believe her story. It could all have been channeled into her mind by the Christian Coalition or the Aryan Nations, who then manipulated this staunch Democratic liberal into confessing her embarrassment on *60 Minutes*.) Whatever the truth of her story—and smoking guns should perhaps not be mentioned right away—she found her life altered once she had gone public. Her car tires ruined . . . her cat gone missing . . . some unexpected attention from a major Clinton fund-raising crony named Nathan Landow . . . nothing you could quite put a name to. As the *Washington Post* unsensationally put it:

> Jarrett Stern, a private investigator, told ABC News in an interview broadcast last night that he was hired for an unspecified project by Landow, a wealthy Maryland developer who has raised hundreds of thousands of dollars for Clinton-Gore campaigns. Stern's lawyer, Edouard Bouquet of Bethesda, told the network his client felt uneasy about what he was asked to do and called Willey, using an alias, to warn her someone was out to do her harm . . .
>
> Stern declined to detail what he had been asked to do in connection with Willey, but he told ABC that he "wholeheartedly" believes that Willey was approached with a menacing message by a stranger jogging near her Richmond home two days before her [Paula] Jones case testimony. Willey has said the man inquired about her children by name, about her missing cat and about whether she'd gotten the tires on her car repaired after they were mysteriously vandalized by someone who drove masses of nails into all four of them. "Don't you get the message?" she has said the man asked.

I. F. Stone once observed that the *Washington Post* was a great newspaper, because you never knew on what page you would find the Page One story. This tale made page ten on the Saturday before the United States Senate called its first witness. Let us imagine and even believe that Ms. Willey and M. Bouquet and Mr. Stern all conspired to tell a lie. You will still have to notice that it is they—lacking state power, or police power, or public-opinion power if it comes to that—who are the "sexual McCarthyites." They are McCarthyites by virtue of having made an allegation. The potential culprits—Mr. Landow or the most powerful man in the world, for whom he raised untold money—are the hapless victims. The charge of McCarthyism aimed at Ms. Willey and her unexpected corroborators could easily have been avoided. They could, after all, have kept quiet. And I almost wish that they had, because then I would not have been told by Gloria Steinem and Betty Friedan and many others that it was Clinton who dared not move outside or even inside his secure executive mansion, for fear of the female stalkers and lynchers and inquisitors who dogged his every step. And outlets like *The Nation* would not have dishonored the memory of McCarthy's victims—many of them men and women of principle who were persecuted for their principles and not for their deeds—by comparing their experience to the contemptible evasions of a cheap crook. Mr. Nate Landow also tried to follow the "McCarthyite" script as much as it lay within his power. Confronted with questions about his leaning on an inconvenient and vulnerable witness, he eagerly sought the protection of the Fifth Amendment against self-incrimination. This and other legal stratagems were not strange to him. Note what Dick Morris said earlier: that when Clinton is in trouble he resorts to the world of soft money for allies. (It is this fact alone that destroys his claim to "privacy," and ties together his public affluence and private squalor.) Nathan Landow is the personification of that shady and manipulative world. He paid a small fortune to have Kathleen Willey flown by private jet from Richmond to his mansion on Maryland's Eastern Shore, where he "pressed her" about her deposition in the Paula Jones case. His fund-raising organization, IMPAC, was and remains a core group in the "money primary" to which Democratic aspirants must submit. (He himself probably prefers Gore to Clinton.) In 1996, he provided a microcosm of the soft-money world in action.

The Cheyenne-Arapaho peoples of Oklahoma have been attempting for years to regain land that was illegally seized from them by the federal government in 1869. Democratic Party fund-raisers persuaded the tribes that an ideal means of gaining attention would be to donate $107,000 to the Clinton-Gore campaign. This contribution secured them a small place at a large lunch with other Clinton donors, but no action. According to the *Washington Post*, a Democratic political operative named Michael Copperthite then petitioned Landow to take up their cause. Landow first required them to register with the consulting firm of Peter Knight, who is Al Gore's chief moneyman and promoter, for a $100,000 retainer and a fee of $10,000 per month. Then he demanded that the Cheyenne-Arapaho sign a development deal with him, handing over 10 percent of all income produced on the recovered land, including the revenues from oil and gas. When news of this nasty deal—which was rejected by the tribes—became public, the Democratic National Committee was forced to return the money and the Senate Committee on Governmental Affairs issued a report describing the "fleecing" of the Indians by "a series of Democratic operators, who attempted to pick their pockets for legal fees, land development and additional contributions."

These are the sort of "Democratic operators" to whom Clinton turns when he needs someone to take care of business. And, of course, Mr. Landow's daughter works at the White House, causing nobody to ask how she got her job. In Clinton's Washington there is always affirmative action for such people.

In the same week as the Landow-Willey revelations, the Court of Appeals decisively reinstated Judge Kenneth Starr's case against Webster Hubbell, his wife, and their two "advisors" for tax evasion. It might be said—probably was said—that when it comes to lying about taxes, "everybody does it." However, Mr. Hubbell's seeming motive in concealing a large tranche of income was not the wish to enjoy its fruits while free of tax. It was—how can one phrase this without sounding like the frightful Inspector Javert?—because he would have had difficulty explaining how he came by the money in the first place. The money, to which I had tried to call attention in my *Los Angeles Times* article a year previously, had been given him by Revlon and other normally tightfisted corporations not unconnected to the soft-money universe inhabited by Clinton. In their reinstatement of the suit, the majority on the Court of Appeals used the dread phrase "hush money" in a rather suggestive, albeit *prima facie*, manner. Many past presidents have appointed sordid underlings at the Department of Justice. One thinks of Bobby Kennedy; one thinks of Edwin Meese. This time, however, almost nobody came forward to say that "they all do it." Perhaps this alibi had become subject, after a grueling workout, to a law that nobody can break with impunity: the law of diminishing returns. There was no sex involved, so Judge Starr was spared the routine yells about his pornographic and prurient obsessions. I continued to chant the slogan I had minted a year previously: "It's not the lipstick traces, stupid. It's the Revlon Connection."

Something like this may have occurred to Senator Russell Feingold of Wisconsin when, only two days later on January 28, he cast the only Democratic vote against dismissing the charges, and also the only

Democratic vote in favor of calling witnesses to the Senate. One says "Democratic" vote, though in point of fact Senator Feingold is the only member of the Senate who is entitled to call himself an independent. In the elections of November 1998, he submitted himself for reelection having announced that he would accept no "soft money" donations. This brave decision, which almost cost him his seat, rallied many Wisconsin voters who had been raised in the grand tradition of LaFollette's midwestern populism—a populism of trustbusting rather than crowd-pleasing. His later Senate vote on impeachment, which represented the misgivings of at least five other senators who were more prudent as well as more susceptible to party discipline, forever negates the unending Clintonoid propaganda about a vast right-wing conspiracy, and also shames all those who were browbeaten into complicity: turned to stone by the waving of Medusa's Heads like Lott and Gingrich, and too slow to realize that such Gorgons were in fact Clinton's once-and-future allies, not his nemesis.

I began this prologue by disclaiming any "hidden agenda." But I think I might as well proclaim the open one. For more than a year, I watched people develop and circulate the most vulgar imaginable conspiracy theories, most of them directed at the work of an Independent Counsel, and all of them part-generated with public funds by a White House that shamelessly and simultaneously whined about its need to resume public business. I heard and saw the most damaging and defamatory muck being readied for the heads and shoulders of women who told, or who might consider telling, the plain truth. I observed, in some quite tasteful Washington surroundings, the incubation of sheer paranoia and rumormongering; most especially the ludicrous claim that Mr. Clinton's departure would lead—had no one read the Constitution?—to the accession of Bob Barr or Pat Robertson to the White House. (I also saw, rather satisfyingly, the same Mr. Robertson, and later all the fund-raisers of the Republican party assembled in conclave in Palm Beach, Florida, as they beseeched the congressional party to leave Mr. Clinton alone, and in general to get with the program.) Not even this consolation, however, could make up for the pro-Clinton and anti-impeachment rally that took place in Washington on December 17, 1998. On that day, as nameless Iraqis died to make a Clinton holiday, and as the most pathetic lies were emitted from the White House, Jesse Jackson and other members of the stage-army of liberalism were gathered on the Capitol steps to wave banners and shout slogans in defense of Clinton's integrity and–yes–privacy. "A Camera in Every Bedroom," said one witless placard, perhaps confusing the off-the-record surveillance conducted by the White House with the on-the-record legal investigation to which Clinton had promised his "full cooperation." As the news of the bombing arrived, and sank in, the poor fools had an impromptu discussion about whether to proceed with their pointless rally, or to adjourn it. They went ahead. It is the argument of all these ensuing pages that the public and private faces of Clintonism are the same, as was proved on that awful day and on many others. It is the hope of these pages, also, that some of the honor of the Left can be rescued from the moral and intellectual shambles of the past seven years, in which the locusts have dined so long and so well.

Among the many occasions on which he telegraphed his personal and political character to the wider world, Clinton's speech at the funeral of Richard Nixon in April 1994 was salient. Speaking as he did after a fatuous harangue from Billy Graham, a piece of self-promoting sanctimony from Henry Kissinger, and a lachrymose performance from Robert Dole, Clinton seemed determined nonetheless to match their standard. There was fatuity in plenty: "Nixon would not allow America to quit the world." There was mawkishness and falsity to spare: "From these humble roots grew the force of a driving dream." There was one useful if alarming revelation: "Even in the final weeks of his life, he gave me his wise counsel, especially in regard to Russia." (One likes to picture Clinton getting pro-Yeltsin phone calls from the old maestro who always guessed the Russians wrong, and who also initiated the ongoing romance between Chinese Stalinism and United States multinational corporations. Perhaps that's what the calls were really about.) However, toward the close of this boilerplated and pharisaic homily, Clinton gave one hostage to fortune, which I scribbled down at the time:

> Today is a day for his family, his friends, and his nation to remember President Nixon's life in totality. To them let me say: May the day of judging President Nixon on anything less than his entire life and career come to a close.

How devoutly I wished that this prayer might be answered: the foul-mouthed anti-Semitism in the Oval Office along with the murder of Allende; the hush money and the Mafia conversations along with the aerial destruction of Indochina; the utter sexlessness along with the incurably dirty mind; the sense of incredulity and self-pity that rose to a shriek when even the least of his offenses was unearthed. I wrote down Clinton's sanctimonious words because I was sure that I would need them one day.

TRIANGULATION

*To have the pleasure and the praise of electioneering ingenuity, and
also to get paid for it, without too much anxiety whether the ingenuity
will achieve its ultimate end, perhaps gives to some select persons a sort
of satisfaction in their superiority to their more agitated fellow-men that
is worthy to be classed with those generous enjoyments—of having the
truth chiefly to yourself, and of seeing others in danger of drowning
while you are high and dry.*

    —George Eliot, *Felix Holt, the Radical*

IT IS TOLD of Huey Long that, contemplating a run for high office, he
summoned the big wads and donors of his great state and enlightened
them thus: "Those of you who come in with me now will receive a big
piece of the pie. Those of you who delay, and commit yourselves later, will
receive a smaller piece of pie. Those of you who don't come in at all will
receive—Good Government!" A touch earthy and plebeian for modern
tastes, perhaps, but there is no doubt that the Kingfish had a primal
understanding of the essence of American politics. This essence, when
distilled, consists of the manipulation of populism by elitism. That elite is
most successful which can claim the heartiest allegiance of the fickle
crowd; can present itself as most "in touch" with popular concerns; can

anticipate the tides and pulses of opinion; can, in short, be the least apparently "elitist." It's no great distance from Huey Long's robust cry of "Every man a king!" to the insipid "inclusiveness" of "Putting People First," but the smarter elite managers have learned in the interlude that solid, measurable pledges have to be distinguished by a "reserve" tag that earmarks them for the bankrollers and backers. They have also learned that it can be imprudent to promise the voters too much.

Unless, that is, the voters should decide that they don't deserve or expect anything. On December 10, 1998, the majority counsel of the House Judiciary Committee, David Schippers, delivered one of the most remarkable speeches ever heard in the precincts. A leathery Chicago law 'n' order Democrat, Mr. Schippers represented the old-style, big-city, blue-collar sensibility which, in the age of Democrats Lite, it had been a priority for Mr. Clinton and his Sunbelt Dixiecrats to discard. The spirit of an earlier time, of a time before "smoking materials" had been banned from the White House, rasped from his delivery. After pedantically walking his hearers through a traditional prosecutor's review of an incorrigible perp (his address could be used in any civics class in the nation, if there were still such things as civics classes), Mr. Schippers paused and said:

> The President, then, has lied under oath in a civil deposition, lied under oath in a criminal grand jury. He lied to the people, he lied to his Cabinet, he lied to his top aides, and now he's lied under oath to the Congress of the United States. *There's no one left to lie to.*

Poor sap, I thought, as I watched this (alone in an unfazed crowd) on a screen at Miami airport. On what wheezing mule did *he* ride into town? So sincere and so annihilating, and so free from distressing sexual graphics, was his forensic presentation that, when it was over, Congressman

John Conyers of the Democratic caucus silkily begged leave of the chair to compliment Mr. Schippers for his efforts. And that was that. Mr. Conyers went back to saying, as he'd said from the first, that the only person entitled to be affronted by the lie was—Mrs. Clinton. Eight days later, the Democratic leadership was telling the whole House that impeachment should not be discussed while the president and commander in chief was engaged in the weighty task of bombing Iraq.

Reluctant though many people still are to accept this conclusion, the two excuses offered by the Democrats are in fact one and the same. Excuse number one, endlessly repeated by liberals throughout 1998, holds that the matter is so private that it can only be arbitrated by the president's chief political ally and closest confidante (who can also avail herself, in case of need, of a presidential pardon). Excuse number two, taken up by the Democratic leadership and the White House as the missiles were striking Baghdad—as they had earlier struck Sudan and Afghanistan— was that the matter was so public as to impose a patriotic duty on every citizen to close ranks and keep silent. (Congressman Patrick Kennedy of Rhode Island, nephew of JFK and RFK and son of "Teddy," no doubt had Judith Exner, Sam Giancana, the Bay of Pigs, and Chappaquiddick in mind when he said that any insinuation of a connection between bombing and impeachment "bordered on treason.")

The task of reviewing the Clinton regime, then, involves the retracing of a frontier between "private" and "public," over a period when "privatization" was the most public slogan of the administration, at home and abroad. It also involves the humbler and more journalistic task of tracing and nailing a series of public lies about secret—not private—matters. Just as the necessary qualification for a good liar is a good memory, so the essential equipment of a would-be lie detector is a good timeline, and a decent archive.

Mr. Schippers was mistaken when he said that there was "no one left to lie to." He was wrong, not in the naive way that we teach children to distinguish truth from falsehood (and what a year it was for "what shall we tell the children?"). In that original, literal sense, he would have been wrong in leaving out Mr. Clinton's family, all of Mr. Clinton's foreign political visitors, and all viewers on the planet within reach of CNN. No, he was in error in that he failed to account for those who *wanted* to be lied to, and those who wished at all costs to believe. He also failed to account for Dick Morris—the sole human being to whom the mendacious president at once confided the truth. (Before, that is, he embarked on a seven-month exploitation of state power and high office to conceal such a "personal" question from others.)

The choice of Mr. Morris as confidante was suggestive, even significant. A cousin of Jules Feiffer and the late Roy Cohn (the Cohn genes were obviously dominant), Mr. Morris served for a long spell as Bill Clinton's pimp. He and Mr. Clinton shared some pretty foul evenings together, bloating and sating themselves at public expense while consigning the poor and defenseless to yet more misery. The kinds of grossness and greed in which they indulged are perfectly cognate with one another—selfish and fleshy and hypocritical and exploitative. "The Monster," Morris called Clinton when in private congress with his whore. "The creep," she called Morris when she could get away and have a decent bath. "The Big Creep" became Monica Lewinsky's post-pet telephone name for the Chief Executive. "The lesser evil" is the title that exalted liberalism has invented to describe this beautiful relationship and all that has flowed from it.

Mr. Morris's most valued gift to the president was his invention—perhaps I should say "coinage"—of the lucrative business known as "triangulation." And this same business has put a new spin on an old ball. The traditional handling of the relation between populism and elitism involves achieving a point of balance between those who support you, and those whom you support. Its classic pitfalls are the accusations that fall between flip and flop, or zig and zag. Its classic advantage is the straight plea for the benefit of the "lesser evil" calculus, which in most modern elections means a straight and preconditioned choice between one and another, or A and B, or Tweedledum and Tweedledee. The most apparently sophisticated and wised-up person, who is well accustomed to saying that "there's nothing to choose between them," can also be heard, under pressure, denouncing abstainers and waverers for doing the work of the extreme Right. In contrast, a potential Perot voter could be identi-fied, in 1992, by his or her tendency to believe simultaneously that (a.) the two main parties were too much alike, resembling two cosily fused but-tocks of the same giant *derrière*, and (b.) that the two matching hemi-spheres spent too much time in fratricidal strife. (Mr. Perot went his supporters one better, by demanding that the United States be run like a corporation—which it already is.) But thus is the corporatist attitude to politics inculcated, and thus failed a movement for a "Third Party" which, in its turn, had failed to recognize that there were not yet two. The same ethos can be imbibed from any edition of the *New York Times*, which invariably uses "partisan" as a pejorative and "bipartisan" as a compli-ment—and this, by the way, in its "objective" and "detached" news columns—but would indignantly repudiate the corollary: namely, that it views favorably the idea of a one-party system.

Let me give respective examples of the practice and theory of triangulation. The practice was captured vividly in a 1999 essay by Robert Reich, Clinton's first-term secretary of labor and one of the small core of liberal policy makers to have been a "Friend of Bill," or FOB, since the halcyon Rhodes Scholarship days of 1969. Mr. Reich here reminisces on the Cabinet discussions he attended in 1996, when the Clinton administration decided to remove many millions of mothers and children from the welfare rolls:

> When, during his 1992 presidential campaign, Bill Clinton vowed to "end welfare as we know it" by moving people "from welfare to work," he presumably did not have in mind the legislation that he signed into law in August 1996. The original idea had been to smooth the passage from welfare to work with guaranteed health care, child care, job training and a job paying enough to live on. The 1996 legislation contained none of these supports—no health care or child care for people coming off welfare, no job training, no assurance of a job paying a living wage, nor, for that matter, of a job at any wage. In effect, what was dubbed welfare "reform" merely ended the promise of help to the indigent and their children which Franklin D. Roosevelt had initiated more than sixty years before.

That is indeed how many of us remember the betrayal of the poor that year. Now here's Reich again, detailing the triangulation aspect of the decision:

> In short, being "tough" on welfare was more important than being correct about welfare. The pledge Clinton had made in 1992, to "end welfare as we know it," and "move people from welfare to work," had fudged the issue. Was this toughness or compassion? It depended on how the words were interpreted. Once elected, Clinton had two years in office with a Congress controlled by Democrats, but, revealingly, did not, during those years, forward to Congress a bill to move people from welfare to work with all the necessary supports, because he feared he could not justify a reform that would, in fact, cost more than the welfare system it was intended to replace.

So, as Mr. Reich goes on to relate in excruciating detail, Mr. Clinton—who was at that stage twenty points ahead in the opinion polls—signed legislation that was more hasty, callous, short-term, and ill-considered than anything the Republicans could have hoped to carry on their own. He thus made sure that he had robbed them of an electoral issue, and gained new access to the very donors who customarily sent money to the other party. (Mr. Reich has good reason to remember this episode with pain. His own wife said to him, when he got home after the vote: "You know, your President is a real asshole.") Yet, perhaps because of old loyalties and his Harvard training in circumlocution, he lacks the brisk ability to synthesize that is possessed by his spouse and also by the conservative theorist David Frum. Writing in Rupert Murdoch's *Weekly Standard* of February 1999, Mr. Frum saw through Clintonism and its triangulations with an almost world-weary ease:

> Since 1994, Clinton has offered the Democratic party a devilish bargain: Accept and defend policies you hate (welfare reform, the Defense of Marriage Act), condone and excuse crimes (perjury, campaign finance abuses) and I'll deliver you the executive branch of government . . . Again since 1994, Clinton has survived and even thrived by deftly balancing between right and left. He has assuaged the Left by continually proposing bold new programs—the expansion of Medicare to 55 year-olds, a national day-care program, the reversal of welfare reform, the hooking up to the Internet of every classroom, and now the socialization of the means of production via Social Security. And he has placated the Right by dropping every one of these programs as soon as he proposed it. Clinton makes speeches, Rubin and Greenspan make policy; the Left gets words, the Right gets deeds; and everybody is content.

I wouldn't describe myself as "content" with the above, or with those so easily satisfied and so credulous that they hailed the welfare bill as a "tough decision" one year, and then gave standing ovations to a cornucopia of vote-purchasing proposals in the "Lewinsky" budget that confirmed Frum's analysis so neatly a week after it was written. He is right, also, to remind people of the Defense of Marriage Act, a straight piece of gaybaiting demagogy and opportunism which Clinton rushed to sign, afterwards purchasing seventy separate "spots" on Christian radio stations in order to brag about the fact. Nobody on the Left has noticed, with Frum's clarity, that it is the Left which swallows the soft promises of Clinton and the Right that demands, and gets, hard guarantees.

Clinton is the first modern politician to have assimilated the whole theory and practice of "triangulation," to have internalized it, and to have deployed it against both his own party and the Republicans, as well as against the democratic process itself. As the political waters dried out and sank around him, the president was able to maintain an edifice of personal power, and to appeal to the credibility of the office as a means of maintaining his own. It is no cause for astonishment that in this "project" he retained the warm support of Arthur Schlesinger, author of *The Imperial Presidency*. However, it might alarm the liberal left to discover that the most acute depiction of presidential imperialism was penned by another clever young neoconservative during the 1996 election. Neatly pointing out that Clinton had been liberated by the eclipse of his congressional party in 1994 to raise his own funds and select his own "private" reelection program, Daniel Casse wrote in the July 1996 *Commentary*:

Today, far from trying to rebuild the party, Clinton is trying to decouple the presidential engine from the Congressional train. *He has learned how the Republicans can be, at once, a steady source of new ideas and a perfect foil.* Having seen where majorities took his party over the past two decades, and what little benefit they brought him in his first months in office, he may even be quietly hoping that the Democrats remain a Congressional minority, and hence that much less likely to interfere with his second term.

Not since Walter Karp analyzed the antagonism between the Carter-era "Congressional Democrats" and "White House Democrats" had anyone so deftly touched on the open secret of party politics. At the close of the 1970s, Tip O'Neill's Hill managers had coldly decided they would rather deal with Reagan than Carter. Their Republican counterparts in the mid-1990s made clear their preference for Clinton over Dole, if not quite over Bush. A flattering profile of Gore, written by the author of *Primary Colors* in the *New Yorker* of October 26, 1998, stated without equivocation that he and Clinton, sure of their commanding lead in the 1996 presidential race, had consciously decided *not* to spend any of their surplus money or time in campaigning for congressional Democrats. This was partly because Mr. Gore did not want to see Mr. Gephardt become Speaker, and thus perhaps spoil his own chances in 2000. But the decision also revealed the privatization of politics, as did the annexation of the fund-raising function by a president who kept his essential alliance with Dick Morris (a conservative Republican and former advisor to Jesse Helms) a secret even from his own staff.

Of course, for unanticipated reasons also having to do with presidential privacy, by the summer of 1998 Mr. Clinton found that he suddenly *did* need partisan support on the Hill. So Casse was, if anything, too subtle. (For Washington reasons that might one day be worth analyzing more minutely, both he and David Frum form part of a conservative subculture that originates in Canada.) He was certainly too flattering to those who had not required anything so subtle in the way of their own seduction. Even as the three-dimensional evidence of "triangulation" was all about them, many of the "core" Democratic constituencies would still settle for the traditional two-dimensional "lesser evil" cajolery: a quick flute of warm and flat champagne before the trousers were torn open ("Liar, liar—pants on fire") and the anxious, turgid member taken out and waved. Two vignettes introduce this "New Covenant":

On February 19, 1996—President's Day—Miss Monica Lewinsky was paying one of her off-the-record visits to the Oval Office. She testified ruefully that no romance, however perfunctory, occurred on this occasion. The president was compelled to take a long telephone call from a sugar grower in Florida named, she thought, "something like Fanuli." In the flat, decidedly nonerotic tones of the Kenneth Starr referral to Congress:

> Ms. Lewinsky's account is corroborated . . . Concerning Ms. Lewinsky's recollection of a call from a sugar-grower named "Fanuli," the President talked with Alfonso Fanjul of Palm Beach, Florida, from 12.42 to 1.04 pm. Mr. Fanjul had telephoned a few minutes earlier, at 12.24 pm. The Fanjuls are prominent sugar growers in Florida.

Indeed, "the Fanjuls are prominent sugar growers in Florida." Heirs of a leading Batista-supporting dynasty in their native Cuba, they are the most prominent sugar growers in the United States. They also possess the distinction of having dumped the greatest quantity of phosphorus waste into the Everglades, and of having paid the heaviest fines for maltreating black stoop laborers from the Dominican Republic ($375,000) and for making illegal campaign contributions ($439,000). As friends of "affir-mative action" for minorities, Alfonso and Jose Fanjul have benefitted from "minority set-aside" contracts for the Miami airport, and receive an annual taxpayer subvention of $65 million in sugar "price supports," which currently run at $1.4 billion yearly for the entire US sugar industry. The brothers have different political sympathies. In 1992, Alfonso was Florida's financial co-chairman for the Clinton presidential campaign. Having been a vice-chairman for Bush/Quayle in 1988, in 1996 Jose was national vice-chairman of the Dole for President Finance Committee.

Alfonso Fanjul called Bill Clinton in the Oval Office, on President's Day (birthday of Washington and Lincoln), and got half an hour of ear time, even as the president's on-staff comfort-woman *du jour* was kept waiting.

Rightly is the Starr referral termed "pornographic," for its exposure of such private intimacies to public view. Even more lasciviously, Starr went on to detail the lipstick traces of the Revlon corporation in finding a well-cushioned post for a minx who was (in the only "exculpatory" statement that Clinton's hacks could seize upon) quoted as saying that "No one ever told me to lie; no one ever promised me a job." How correct the liberals are in adjudging these privy topics to be prurient and obscene. And how apt it is, in such a crisis, that a Puritan instinct for decent reticence should come to Clinton's aid.

My second anecdote concerns a moment in the White House, which was innocently related to me by George Stephanopoulos. It took place shortly after the State of the Union speech in 1996 when the president, having already apologized to the "business community" for burdening it with too much penal taxation, had gone further and declared that "the era of big government is over." There was every reason, in the White House at that stage, to adopt such a "triangulation" position and thereby deprive the

Republicans of an old electoral mantra. But Stephanopoulos, prompted by electoral considerations as much as by any nostalgia for the despised New Deal, proposed a rider to the statement. Ought we not to add, he ventured, that we do not propose a policy of "Every Man For Himself"? To this, Ann Lewis, Clinton's director of communications, at once riposted scornfully that she could not approve any presidential utterance that used "man" to mean mankind. Ms. Lewis, the sister of Congressman Barney Frank and a loudly self-proclaimed feminist in her own right, was later to swallow, or better say retract, many of her own brave words about how "sex is sex," small print or no small print, and to come out forthrightly for the libidinous autonomy (and of course, "privacy") of the Big Banana. And thus we have the introduction of another theme that is critical to our story. *At all times, Clinton's retreat from egalitarian or even from "progressive" positions has been hedged by a bodyguard of political correctness.*

In his awful $2.5 million Random House turkey, artlessly entitled *Behind the Oval Office*, Dick Morris complains all the way to the till. "Triangulation," he writes, "is much misunderstood. It is not merely splitting the difference between left and right." This accurate objection—we are talking about a three-card monte and not an even split—must be read in the context of its preceding sentence: "Polls are not the instrument of the mob; they offer the prospect of leadership wedded to a finely-calibrated measurement of opinion."

By no means—let us agree once more with Mr. Morris—are polls the instrument of the mob. The mob would not know how to poll itself, nor could it afford the enormous outlay that modern polling requires. (Have you ever seen a poll asking whether or not the Federal Reserve is too secretive? Who would pay to ask such a question? Who would know how to answer it?) Instead, the polling business gives the patricians an idea of what the mob is thinking, and of how that thinking might be changed or, shall we say, "shaped." It is the essential weapon in the mastery of populism by the elite. It also allows for "fine calibration," and for capsules of "message" to be prescribed for variant constituencies.

In the 1992 election, Mr. Clinton raised discrete fortunes from a gorgeous mosaic of diversity and correctness. From David Mixner and the gays he wrung immense sums on the promise of lifting the ban on homosexual service in "the military"—a promise he betrayed with his repellent "don't ask, don't tell" policy. From a variety of feminist circles he took even larger totals for what was dubbed "The Year of the Woman," while he and his wife applauded Anita Hill for her bravery in "speaking out" about funny business behind the file cabinets. Some Jews—the more conservative and religious ones, to be precise—were massaged by Clinton's attack on George Bush's policy of withholding loan guarantees from the ultra-chauvinist Yitzhak Shamir. For the first time since Kennedy's day, Cuban-American extremists were brought into the Democratic tent by another attack on Bush from the right—this time a promise to extend the embargo on Cuba to third countries. Each of these initiatives yielded showers of fruit from the money tree. At the same time, Clinton also came to office seeming to promise universal health care, a post-Cold War sensitivity to human rights, a decent outrage about the Bush/Baker/Eagleburger cynicism in Bosnia, China, and Haiti, and on top of all that, "a government that looked more like America." Within weeks of the "Peoples' Inaugural" in January 1993, Interior Secretary Bruce Babbitt arranged a deal on the Everglades with the Fanjul family, leaving Al Gore's famous "environmentalist" fans seething and impotent at the first of many, many disappointments.

TWO

CHAMELEON IN BLACK AND WHITE

IN HIS HOT YOUTH in the 1960s, Bill Clinton had been, on his own account, a strong supporter of the civil rights movement. Recalling those brave days during the April 1997 anniversary celebrations of Jackie Robinson's victory over Jim Crow in baseball, he told an invited audience:

> When I was a young person, both I and my family thought that the seg-
> regation which dominated our part of the country was wrong ... So he
> was like—he was fabulous evidence for people in the South, when we
> were all arguing over the integration of the schools, the integration of
> all public facilities, basically the integration of our national life.
> Whenever some bigot would say something, you could always cite
> Jackie Robinson ... You know, if you were arguing the integration side
> of the argument, you could always play the Jackie Robinson card and
> watch the big husky redneck shut up [here the transcript shows a
> chuckle] because there was nothing they could say.

Actually, there would have been something the big husky redneck could have said. "Huh?" would have about covered it. Or perhaps, "Run along, kid." Jackie Robinson—a lifelong Republican—broke the color line in baseball in 1947, when Clinton was one. He retired from the game in 1956, when Clinton was nine. The Supreme Court had decided in favor of school integration two years before that. Perhaps the seven-year-old boy wonder did confront the hefty and the white-sheeted with his piping treble, but not even the fond memoirs of his doting mama record the fact.

As against that, at the close of Mr. Clinton's tenure as governor, Arkansas was the only state in the union that did not have a civil rights statute. It seems safe to say this did not trouble his conscience too heavily. Let us consult the most sympathetic biography of Clinton ever published, *The President We Deserve*, by the excellent British correspondent Martin Walker of *The Guardian*. (His book was simultaneously published in London, under the even happier title *The President They Deserve*.) Described as "truly sensational" by Sidney Blumenthal in the *New Yorker* (and thus by a reviewer who, we may be sure, intended no invasion of privacy), Walker's account of Clinton's rise covers his electoral defeat in Arkansas in 1980. Clinton had begun his two years at the State House by inviting the venomous old segregationist Orval Faubus, the former governor of Arkansas, to a place of honor at the inaugural ceremony (a step that might have caused Jackie Robinson to raise an eyebrow), but not even this was enough to protect him against vulgar, local accusations of "nigger-loving." The crunch moment came in the dying days of the Carter administration, when Cuban "Mariel boatlift" refugees were stuffed into an emergency holding pen at Fort Chafee, and later protested against their confinement. As Walker phrases it: "the ominous black-and-white shots of dark-skinned Cuban rioters against white-faced police and Arkansans had carried a powerful subliminal message." The boyish governor knew what to do at once. (His conversion to friendship with Cuban refugees did not come until he met the Fanjul brothers.) He vowed to prevent any more Cubans from landing on Arkansas soil, and declared loudly that he would defy the federal government "even if they bring the whole United States Army down here." This echo of the rebel yell was correctly described by Paul Greenberg, columnist for the *Arkansas Democrat-Gazette*, as "a credible imitation of Orval E. Faubus." Walker tactfully omits that revealing moment, but goes on to describe, with insights from the Clinton inner circle, the conclusion that Bill and Hillary drew from the ensuing reverse at the polls: "The lessons were plain: never be outnegatived again."

Perhaps, like the earlier TV impressions he cites, this dictum only occurs to Mr. Walker in the "subliminal" sense. But its provenance is well established. George Wallace, defeated by a less polished racist in an electoral tussle in long-ago Alabama, swore in public "never to be out-niggered again." This slogan was well known, and well understood, in all the former states of the Old Confederacy. And after 1980, Clinton clearly began to evolve a "Southern strategy" of his own.

In the 1992 run for the Democratic nomination, that strategy became plain for anyone willing to see it. Clinton took care to have himself photographed at an all-white golf club, and also standing at a prison farm photo-op, wearing his shades in the sunshine while a crowd of uniformed black convicts broke rocks in the sun. Taxed with long-time membership in the "exclusive" golf club—"inclusiveness" being only a buzz-word away—Clinton calmly replied that the club's "staff and facilities" were integrated, a "legally accurate" means of stating the obvious fact that at least the hired help was colored. He invited himself to Jesse Jackson's Rainbow Coalition conference, and there went out of his way (having alerted reporters in the meantime) to pick a fight with the inflammatory rap lyrics of Sister Souljah. Ambushed in this style, the Reverend Jackson exasperatedly—and rather presciently—described the hungry young candidate as "just an appetite." Clinton fashioned an electoral mantra out of the promise to "end welfare as we know it," making the morals of the underclass into the salient issue and none-too-subtly leaving the hue of that class to the imagination. Most memorably—I say this in spite of the fact that so many people have succeeded in forgetting it—he quit the thick of the New Hampshire primary, in January 1992, in order to fly back to Arkansas and give personal supervision to the execution of Rickey Ray Rector.

Rector was a black lumpen failure, convicted of a double murder, who had shot himself in the head on arrest and achieved the same result as a frontal lobotomy would have done. He understood his charge and trial and sentence not at all. Nursed back to life and condemned to death, he had spent a decade on Death Row in Cummins prison. His execution number came up in a week when Clinton, according to one report of the poll numbers, had lost twelve points as a result of the Gennifer Flowers disclosures. These two "numbers" were accordingly made to intersect. In 1988, Clinton had backed the ludicrous presidential campaign of Michael Dukakis, a personal coward and political dolt who had lost an easy argument about capital punishment in a public debate with George Bush, and who had also suffered from a sleazy "subliminal" campaign about a dusky parole-breaking rapist named Willie Horton. Official Democratic folklore (which also carefully forgot that Horton had first been used by Senator Al Gore as a weapon against Dukakis in the primaries) coagulated around the view that no candidate should ever be out-Hortoned again. The mass media ministered to this "perception." In the week of the Flowers revelations, *Time* magazine helpfully inquired: "Suppose Clinton does sew up the nomination by mid-March and the Republicans discover a Willie Horton in his background?" The quasi-sentient Rickey Ray Rector was to provide the perfect rebuttal to such annoying speculations about the governor's credibility.

A few columnists—the late Murray Kempton, Jimmy Breslin, and your humble servant among them—commented with disgust on this human sacrifice, but the press pack preferred to use Clinton's successful lying about Gennifer Flowers as the test of his fitness for high office. It was not until more than a year later that the whole story of Rector's last days was recounted by Marshall Frady in a long essay in the *New Yorker*. Served his traditional last meal, Rector had left the pecan pie on the side of the tray, as he incoherently explained to his queasy guards, "for later." Strapped to a gurney, he had tried to help his executioners find a viable vein (his blood vessels were impaired by an antipsychotic drug) before they inflicted a "cut-down" and slashed the crook of his arm with a scalpel to insert a catheter. It seems he thought they were physicians trying to help him. For many poor Americans of all colors, jail is the only place where doctors, lawyers, teachers, and chaplains are, however grudgingly, made available to them. An hour was spent on the cut-down process, before the death-giving chemicals could kick in. Warden Willis Sargent, a tough former Army non-com, was assailed by misgivings as the deadline approached. "Rickey's a harmless guy," he said. "This is not something I want to do." The police department witness, Lieutenant Rodney Pearson (Rector had shot a cop) found himself having second thoughts as he watched an obviously gravely retarded and uncomprehending prisoner being subjected to the "strap-down." The chaplain, Dennis Pigman, resigned from the prison system shortly afterwards, saying: "I hate murder. I hate murderers. But to execute children? What was done to Rickey Ray

Rector was in itself, absolutely, a crime. A horrible crime. We're not supposed to *execute children*."

Well, that of course depends on the needs of the hour, and the require-
ments of a "New Democrat." Most nauseating, in Mr. Frady's account, was
the lip-biting conduct of Governor Clinton himself. At all times, he pretended—to Rector's lawyer Jeff Rosenzweig and to others who managed to
reach him in the closing moments—that this was a very painful moment for
him *personally*. But that same affectation exposed itself when he received a
telephone call from his friend Carolyn Staley, director of the Governor's
Commission on Adult Literacy. Hearing on the radio that Rector's execution
was stalled by the snag of finding a usable vein, she telephoned her friend Bill
and he called her back and—well, I'll let Mr. Frady tell it:

> She told him, "I just wanted to let you know that I'm praying for you
> about the execution tonight," and he replied in a groan, "It's just awful.
> Just terrible, terrible." As she recalls it now, "I heard in his voice a self—a
> depth of anguish—I'd never, never heard in him before." She then told
> him, "You know, he's not even dead yet." "*What?*" she remembers him
> exclaiming. "*What?*" From his startlement, it was obvious to her that the
> conference in which he had been absorbed had not exactly been a "blow
> by blow" account of Rector's fate . . . Staley then told him, "Bill, I'm so
> sorry. We've had two executions this week, haven't *we*." She meant the
> Flowers allegations. "He just groaned," she remembers, and they moved
> on to discussing that topic. Ultimately, she says, the conversation wound
> up "much more about the Gennifer Flowers matter" than about what was
> happening to Rector at that moment down at Cummins.

Easy to believe. One is compelled to acknowledge the versatility, and
the quick-change between ostentatious pain-feeling and everyday political instinct. It was during those same closing moments that Clinton and

his spouse decided on their celebrated *60 Minutes* strategy, and left Little Rock refreshed for a round of campaign and fund-raising appearances where the "character question" would be conveniently limited to a choice between a dizzy blonde and a "strong woman." This moment deserves to be remembered for a number of reasons: first because it introduces a Clintonian mannerism of *faux* "concern" that has since become tediously familiar, second because it illuminates his later attitude toward matters racial, and matters penal, and third because it marks the first of many times that Clinton would deliberately opt for death as a means of distraction from sex.

I followed Clinton from New Hampshire to Arkansas to California to New York that season, noticing with subdued admiration the ways in which his fans and staffers would recommend him in private. "He's already won the two invisible primaries," one was often told by the wised-up, "the money primary and the polling primary." This was true enough; the "donor community" had adopted him early, and the pundits likewise conferred the charismatic title of "front-runner" before a single New Hampshire ballot had been cast. Clinton actually lost that primary, which pundits and other political chin-pullers had hitherto described as a *sine qua non*, but it was then decided, in the circles that "counted," that this didn't count this time. Most amazing though, was the frequently heard observation that Clinton, as a Southerner, "understood black people." This extraordinary piece of condescension was convertible currency, as it turned out, because of the jolt delivered to consensus by the disorders in Los Angeles. Nervous voters everywhere found Bush's response to be insufficiently fuzzy. Clinton, it was widely assumed, would be more "caring" and "healing." The impression—again "subliminal"—helped him considerably. But an impression it was. Clinton gave the City of the Angels a wide berth, and limited his comments to some platitudes, taken from the play-book of neoconservatism, about the "culture of poverty" in South Central.

That very idiom—naturally concerned yet nonetheless strict—was to become the substratum of his now-celebrated "comfort level" with black Americans while in office. Obviously on good personal terms with Vernon Jordan and Ron Brown and Mike Espy (one of them a conduit to Pamela Harriman's opulent PAC, one of them the genius fund-extorter of the Democratic National Committee, and one of them a long-time friend of Tyson Foods), Clinton also rocked to Aretha Franklin on the Mall during his inauguration and invited Maya Angelou to deliver a piece of dog-gerel poetry at the ceremony itself. Well versed in the cant of Southern Baptist rhetorical uplift, the new president was capable of working the crowd at black church services, just as, infinitely protean in devotional matters, he never looked out of place standing next to Billy Graham or Mother Teresa. However, there were four occasions when push, to employ an old political cliche, came to shove.

The first of these moments took place when Clinton proposed Dr. Lani Guinier to head the Civil Rights Division of the Justice Department. Dr. Guinier was and is a legal scholar of some distinction. She and her husband had invited the Clintons to their wedding, and had helped introduce them to polite society on Martha's Vineyard. She had helped calm Jesse Jackson and other black leaders after Clinton had staged the Sister Souljah headline grab-ber. ("You got your story," Jackson had crisply told George Stephanopoulos and Paul Begala as he left the platform on that occasion.) However, in essays for the *Yale Law Review* and other journals, Dr. Guinier had made the unpar-donable mistake of thinking aloud about proportional representation in Dixie. After being fed a misleading attack circulated by Abigail Thernstrom, a neoconservative opponent of affirmative action, the Republican Right pounced, and arraigned her as a "Quota Queen" opposed to majority–or at any rate majoritarian–rule. This was a slander. Dr. Guinier had expressed her opposition to quotas on principle, and had actually written on the need for electoral "weighting" arrangements to protect the *white* minority in South Africa. She was also in the process of making an excellent impression on the Republican senators who had originally believed the first-draft briefing papers circulated by extremists about her. None of this prevented Clinton's peremptory withdrawal, in June 1993, of her nomination:

> At the time of the nomination, I had not read her writings. I wish I had. The problem is that this battle will be waged based on her academic writings. And I cannot fight a battle that I know is divisive, that is an uphill battle, that is distracting to the country, if I do not believe in the ground of the battle. That is the only problem.

These were early days, and the delight of parsing a Clinton paragraph had not yet attained to the joy it has since become. Still, it is striking to note that Clinton did not "believe in the ground of the battle." The ground of the battle, according to him, was "her academic writings." And these awkward texts he had, on his own admission, "not read." There was, in the tenses, a very slight suggestion that he might have read them *since* the nomination, in which case he could have discerned for himself, as a Yale Law graduate and a member of the bar, that what was being said about his friend was literally and figuratively untrue. But even that suggestion was overshadowed by a declared refusal to involve himself with anything that was "divisive," or that might involve "an uphill battle," or that could "distract the country." And this reluctance in turn would seem to exclude any very staunch commitment to racial equality, let alone to facing down "big husky rednecks" in the Deep South, as six-or-was-it-nine-year-old Bill had once known how to do.

The grace note was left to Mrs. Clinton, who happened to pass by Dr. Guinier in a corridor just as the news of the administration's retreat was sinking in. Waving to her old friend without breaking stride, the First Lady managed to blurt the words "Hey kiddo!," adding ten paces later that she was "half an hour late for a luncheon" before pushing on and leaving her to reflect. A final insult was also delivered, and recorded in Dr. Guinier's extremely literate and persuasive memoir, *Lift Every Voice*:

> We had tried to get Vernon Jordan to come. Vernon had told me he could be helpful with Senator Alan Simpson. During a relaxed, one-on-one meeting in his law office, Vernon had offered to meet or call Simpson on my behalf should that become necessary. When Vernon was subsequently asked to follow up with Simpson, he reportedly said, "I don't do that kind of thing."

Oh but he does, he does . . . When the rich and spoiled daughters of donors and fund-raisers are given affirmative-action jobs at the White House, Mr. Jordan can't do enough of that kind of thing.

White House aversion to the "divisive" may have been genuine in its own terms, because the important civil rights post at Justice went unfilled for more than twelve months (nothing divisive about that, one is compelled to notice) before going to Derval Patrick. Mr. Patrick, who might without unfairness be described as one of the less prominent members of the administration, found himself short of "access" and "input" and other crucial resources. In January 1995, he decided not to accompany Mr. Clinton to Dr. King's birthplace in Atlanta for the annual birthday commemoration. He had discovered that the president's speech would not allude to civil rights, but would take the form of a stern lecture on good behavior to young black men. Mr. Patrick had failed to divine Mr. Clinton's original and essential "message," dating back to his days at the Democratic Leadership Council: It is time for some people in society to set a good example of moral continence, industry, and thrift. Since this admonition is not going to be delivered to the Fanjuls, or to Roger Tamraz, or to the Hollywood "benefit nights," it may as well be orated, with suitable notice for the networks, to a captive audience of another sort. (In *The Importance of Being Earnest*, Algernon languidly observes that if the lower orders will not set an example, it is difficult to see the point of them.)

Clinton's next test of loyalty to black friends and colleagues involved his surgeon-general, Dr. Joycelyn Elders. Never popular with the phalanx that concentrated around the "Contract With America," this lady was to make two mistakes. Charged with responsibility for matters of public health, she asked whether it might be wise to lift the prohibition, not of soft narcotics, but on any debate about decriminalizing them. The striking thing about Mr. Clinton's rapid response was not his stony opposition to decriminalization but his vehement opposition to the merest mention of the topic. It was the debate, not the proposal, that he forbade. In effect, he told his surgeon-general to shut up. That was, had she but known how to recognize it, her "first strike." Nor was she allowed three. At another public forum, where the subject was sexual well-being among American teenagers, Dr. Elders proposed an open discussion of masturbation, as well as of the existing choice between latex sheaths and abstinence. The presidential firing that followed was swift and peremptory. It was as if the good doctor had publicly defiled the temple of her own body. One feels almost laughably heavy-footed in pointing out that Mrs.

Clinton's prim little book, *It Takes a Village*, proposes sexual abstinence for the young, and that the president was earnestly seconding this very proposal while using an impressionable intern as the physical rather than moral equivalent of a blow-up doll.

The third instance—one exempts altogether the "National Initiative" of conversation about race and racism, which withered on the vine and lost the president's attention altogether—concerns Peter and Marian Wright Edelman. With a near peerless record in the civil rights movement (it was Marian Wright Edelman who first introduced Hillary Clinton to Vernon Jordan), this couple had worked unstintingly for Democratic liberalism and in the conviction that children should not suffer for the blunders or crimes or sheer failures of their parents. By 1996, with welfarism and welfare mothers the main, if not sole, political culprits in a social landscape rife with every other kind of depradation, this simple concept seemed as sinister as Sweden—almost as sinister as socialism itself. Going further than any Republican president had ever dared venture, and prompted every day by Dick Morris, who considered this boldness to be the essence of triangulation, Clinton proposed that a sixty-year federal commitment to children in poverty be scrapped, and the whole problem be referred to the budget-conscious fifty states. A provision in the bill mandated that if a woman would not or could not give the name of her child's father, or objected to this invasion of her privacy, she could be stricken from the welfare rolls.

Shortly after the November elections, I was given an eyewitness account of the White House conclave at which the Clintonoid inner circle made its decision to sign the welfare bill. Not all the positions taken at this "defining" meeting were predictable: the sternest and longest holdout against the act was mounted by Treasury Secretary Robert Rubin, though I suppose he did have reasons of New York exceptionalism for taking this stand. Another detail that my informant let fall is worth "sharing." There was, he said, one argument that carried no weight in the room. This was the view, put forward by Mr. Morris, that failure to sign the bill would result in a Republican victory in November. "Dick won," he said, "but not because he persuaded anyone of that."

On September 11, Peter Edelman, after long service at the Department of Health and Human Services, had tendered his resignation. This gave him the distinction, along with two colleagues who resigned at the same time and for the same reasons, of being the only example of a departure on principle from either Clinton administration. Edelman resigned, not just because of the policy decision itself, but because of the extreme cynicism that lay behind it.

At about the same time, Dick Morris was caught by a tabloid newspaper in the Jefferson Hotel, wasting his substance (and perhaps other peoples' too) with harlots and high living. No relativist words about privacy or consenting adults were spoken on this occasion: it was an election season, after all, and the president dropped him from the team without compunction. But in compensation, he and his wife publicly lamented Mr. Morris's fate, and wished him back very soon (and got him back even sooner, though without advising anybody of the fact). I chanced to run into Peter Edelman at about the same time, and asked him out of curiosity: "Did you get any calls from Bill or Hillary asking you to stay, or saying they're sorry you went?" No, Mr. Edelman had not. Like Lani Guinier, who never heard from her old friends the Clintons again (apart from a machine-generated Christmas card), he had been triangulated out of political existence.

Mike Espy, another black Clinton appointment, was secretary for agriculture until he was accused of taking favors and gratuities from the agribusiness interests he was supposed to regulate and supervise. An application from the special prosecutor to investigate the whole pattern of political donations from Don Tyson and Tyson Foods was immediately rejected by Attorney General Janet Reno, a biddable mediocrity whose tenure at the Justice Department was itself something of a scandal. As a consequence, the evidence against Espy became rather a matter of nickels and dimes, and he was eventually acquitted. With the acquittal secure, Clinton found the courage to offer congratulations. But Mr. Espy was not as impressed as he might have been by this display of summer-soldier solidarity. He had, after all, been fired from the Cabinet as soon as the charges against him had been made. And Clinton had delegated the firing to his chief of staff Leon Panetta, afterwards keeping his distance entirely. Mr. Espy could have consoled himself on one score, however. There could be no question of any discrimination in his case. His boss would always abandon a friend in trouble, regardless of race, color, or creed. Only men like Webster Hubbell received continued, solicitous attention, at least in the period elapsing between their indictments and the expiry of the statute of limitations.

During the 1990 midterm elections, the most blatantly racist electoral appeal was offered by Senator Jesse Helms of North Carolina. Nobody who was anywhere near a liberal mailing list between the years 1980 and 1996 could have avoided a solicitation from various Democrat-sponsored coalitions against "The New Right's Prince of Darkness." By hauling up buckets of sludge from the deepest wells of the racist and fundamentalist Old Confederacy, Helms had made himself the most visible and unapologetic target. But his last-ditch TV advertisement of 1994 became the standard by which the liberals measured cynicism. On screen, a pair of work-worn white hands were seen opening an envelope, and then sadly crumpling the enclosed missive. "You needed that job," said the sorrowful voice-over, "but it had to go to a minority." But I have found that most liberals are still shocked to hear that the author of the "white hands" TV incitement was—Dick Morris.

They have no right to be shocked. By late 1998, it was being openly said in Democratic and liberal quarters that the wronged President Clinton was being lynched, yes, just as Clarence Thomas had once been lynched, by a posse of big and husky rednecks. On the floor of the House, with the evident approval of the Democratic leadership, Maxine Waters said that the defense of this wronged man was the moral equivalent of the fight against slavery and segregation. During the Senate trial, the White House fielded a young black woman attorney, Cheryl Mills, to make essentially the same point. And when the trial managers failed to call the president's secretary Betty Currie, the race card was played yet again. Clinton's spinners successfully spread the word that the senators feared to question a shy and dignified black lady (whose life, incidentally, had been made a hell of lawyer's bills by the actions of her boss) lest she break down and cry. There was something brilliantly sordid about this last innuendo: nobody knew better than the White House that a private deal had been made between senators Lott and Daschle to restrict the number of witnesses to three. And these potentates had decided that Sidney Blumenthal was a better test of Clinton's human shield than a fragile secretary.

This sort of tactic works well enough for the daily news cycle, and for the latest opinion poll. But it may not be enough to satisfy the high-minded that they are, as ever, on the right side. (Or, to put it another way, that the side they are on is the right one.) The niche market of the intellectuals—once described by Harold Rosenberg as "the herd of independent minds"—was to be served by its own designated hero, the former playwright Arthur Miller. Writing in the *New York Times* on October 15, 1998, the author of *The Crucible* shared the following thoughts:

> Witch-hunts are always spooked by women's horrifying sexuality awakened by the superstud Devil. In Europe, where tens of thousands perished in the hunts, broadsides showed the Devil with two phalluses, one above the other. And of course mankind's original downfall came about when the Filthy One corrupted the mother of mankind. In Salem, witch-hunting ministers had the solemn duty to examine women's bodies for signs of the "Devil's Marks"—a suggestion of webbing, perhaps, between the toes, a mole behind an ear or between the legs, or a bite mark somewhere. I thought of this wonderfully holy exercise when Congress went pawing through Kenneth Starr's fiercely exact report on the President's intimate meetings with Monica Lewinsky. I guess nothing changes all that much.

Oh but surely, Mr. Miller, some things have changed? Just to take your observations in order, Miss Paula Jones—the witch or bitch in this case, depending on whether you take the verdict of James Carville or Edward Bennett—did not accuse the president of flaunting two phalluses. Indeed, she implied that it would have taken two of his phalluses to make one normal one, which could even be part of the reason why he paid her the sum of $840,000 to keep quiet. (This payment involved dipping into the "blind trust" maintained by his wife, and perhaps put aside for a rainy day after her success in the cattle-futures and other markets.) Stepping lightly over this point, Mr. Clinton has admitted to nothing at all *except* the defilement of his relations with his wife and the mother of his daughter, and has used the pair of them for Bible-bearing photo-ops on every Sunday morning since then. No woman's body was probed by the inquisitors of the Starr team, though there do seem to have been some very close examinations—and even a few bite marks, according to some—visited by the chief executive on certain females. Rather, the Starr team examined the body of the world's most powerful man, as a result of a legal process that had been initiated by one of the world's least powerful women and seconded on a 9–0 vote by the Supreme Court. You are right in describing the Starr findings as "fiercely exact," because not even the Alpha male defendant has challenged them. Yet Congress had no choice but to "paw through" said findings, which were lawfully commissioned by the Alpha male's usually complicit female attorney general. And the evidence there discovered—necessarily a bit grungy, as is common with investigations of sexual harassment, and with evasions of same—consisted not of "Devil's Marks" but of matching DNA.

The above does not prove that Clinton is The Evil One, but it does prove beyond a peradventure that Arthur Miller is The Stupid One. Would he let it go at that? He would not. Digging a deeper ditch for himself, and handing up the shovel, he continued:

> Then there is the color element. Mr. Clinton, according to Toni Morrison, the Nobel Prize-winning novelist, is our first black President, the first to come from the broken home, the alcoholic mother, the under-the-bridge shadows of our ranking systems.

Thus, we may have lost the mystical power to divine diabolism, but we can still divine blackness by the following symptoms: broken homes, alcoholic mothers, under-the-bridge habits, and (presumable from the rest of Arthur Miller's senescent musings) the tendency to sexual predation and to shameless perjury about same. I can remember a time when Ronald Reagan's genial caricature of the vodka-soaked welfare mother was considered "offensive" by all those with OK opinions, if only because half the white children in America had been brought up by caring nannies—sober and decent black ladies—who had to tend to their own children when they had finished with their day jobs. But in Reagan's day, the children of the most shiftless white or black mother were still guaranteed a federal minimum. And Reagan would never have dared to stage a *Primary Colors* photoop execution—if only for fear of the fulminant liberal response that Clinton avoided. In the asinine remarks of Miller, the Left's hero of the 1950s, political correctness has achieved its own negation.

In July 1998, during the third and last televised forum of his national "dialogue" on race, Clinton was confronted by the Native American poet and novelist Sherman Alexie, who complained that many of his fellows were still living in the United States' version of the Third World. Responding, Clinton announced that his grandmother had been one-quarter Cherokee. This claim, never advanced before, would, if true, have made him the first Native American president. It didn't wash with Alexie, who later observed that people "are always talking about race in coded language. What they will do is come up to me and say they're Cherokee." Clinton did his best to be the first to laugh. Within weeks, Clinton's symbolic pandering brought him a balloon of black sympathy in the bell curves of the opinion polls. He had hired Jesse Jackson to replace Billy Graham as Minister of choice and to counsel his stricken daughter, and he had closed his "atonement" appeal for the November 1998 elections at a fund-raiser in a black church in Baltimore, Maryland—an unconstitutional action for which he was later sued by Americans United for the Separation of Church and State. By these last-minute improvisations, he had, without calling any undue attention to the fact, become the first president to play the race card both ways—once traditionally and once, so to speak, in reverse. His opportunist defenders, having helped him with a reversible chameleonlike change in the color of his skin, still found themselves stuck with the content of his character.

THREE

THE POLICY COUP

HISTORY DOES NOT record the nature of the luncheon for which Hillary Clinton was so late that she could only spare a "Hey kiddo" for an endangered and isolated friend. But at that stage of 1993, she was, to outward appearances, all radiant energy and business in pursuit of health care for all. Many initiatives were put "on hold" because they were thought subordinate to this overarching objective. The late Les Aspin, Clinton's luckless and incompetent secretary of defense, once told me that he had planned to make a brief personal appearance in Sarajevo, in order to keep some small part of the empty campaign promise made by Clinton to the Bosnians, but had been ordered to stay at home lest attention be distracted from "Hillary's health-care drive." To this day, many people believe that the insurance companies torpedoed a worthwhile if somewhat complex plan. In numerous self-pitying accounts, the First Lady and her underlings have spoken with feeling on the point. Perhaps you remember the highly successful "Harry and Louise" TV slots, where a painfully average couple pondered looming threats to their choice of family physician. As Mrs. Clinton put it in a fighting speech in the fall of 1993:

> I know you've all seen the ads. You know, the kind of homey kitchen ads where you've got the couple sitting there talking about how the President's plan is going to take away choice and the President's plan is going to narrow options, and then that sort of heartfelt sigh by that woman at the end, "There must be a better way"—you know, you've seen that, right? What you *don't* get told in the ad is that it is paid for by insurance companies. It is time for you and for every American to stand up and say to the insurance industry: "Enough is enough, we want our health-care system back!"

It is fortunate for the Clintons that this populist appeal was unsuccessful. Had the masses risen up against the insurance companies, they would have discovered that the four largest of them—Aetna, Prudential, Met Life, and Cigna—had helped finance and design the "managed-competition" scheme which the Clintons and their Jackson Hole Group had put forward in the first place. These corporations, and the Clintons, had also decided to exclude from consideration, right from the start, any "single-payer" or "Canadian-style" solution. A group of doctors at the Harvard Medical School, better known as Physicians for a National Health Program, devised a version of single-payer which combined comprehensive coverage, to include the 40 million uninsured Americans, with free choice in the selection of physicians. The Congressional Budget Office certified this plan as the most cost-effective on offer. Dr. David Himmelstein, one of the leaders of the group, met Mrs. Clinton in early 1993. It became clear, in the course of their conversation, that she wanted two things simultaneously: the insurance giants "on board," and the option of attacking said giants if things went wrong. Dr. Himmelstein laid out the advantages of his plan, and pointed out that some 70 percent of the public had shown support for such a scheme. "David," said the First Lady, before wearily dismissing him, "tell me something interesting."

The "triangulation" went like this. Harry and Louise sob-story ads were paid for by the Health Insurance Association of America (HIAA), a group made up of the smaller insurance providers. The major five insurance corporations spent even more money to support "managed competition" and to buy up HMOs as the likeliest investment for the future. The Clintons demagogically campaigned against the "insurance industry," while backing—and with the backing of—those large fish that were preparing to swallow the minnows. This strategy, invisible to the media (which in those days rather liked the image of Hillary versus the fat cats), was neatly summarized by Patrick Woodall of Ralph Nader's Public Citizen:

> The managed competition-style plan the Clintons have chosen virtually guarantees that the five largest health-insurance companies—Aetna, Prudential, Met Life, Cigna, and The Travelers—will run the show in the health-care system.

And Robert Dreyfuss of Physicians for a National Health Program added:

> The Clintons are getting away with murder by portraying themselves as opponents of the insurance industry. It's only the small fry that oppose their plan. Under any managed-competition scheme, the small ones will be pushed out of the market very quickly.

As indeed it was to prove. Having come up with a plan that embodied the worst of bureaucracy and the worst of "free enterprise," and having seen it fail abjectly because of its abysmal and labyrinthine complexity, the Clintons dropped the subject of health care for good. The president threw away the pen that he told the Congress he would only use to sign a bill for universal and portable coverage, and instead proposed no bill or remedy at all. Thus was squandered a political consensus on health care which had taken a decade to build up, and which had been used by the Clintons as a short-term electoral vehicle against a foundering George Bush. Since they had been gambling, in effect, with other peoples' chips, the First Couple felt little pain.

The same could not be said for the general population, or for the medical profession, which was swiftly annexed by huge HMOs like Columbia Sunrise. Gag rules for doctors, the insistence on no-choice allocations of primary "caregivers," and actual bonuses paid to physicians and nurses and emergency rooms that denied care, or even restricted access to new treatments, soon followed. So did the exposure of extraordinary levels of corruption in the new health-care conglomerates. Until the impeachment crisis broke, no comment was made by the administration about any of these phenomena, which left most patients and most doctors measurably worse off than they had been in 1992.

By the fall of 1998, with his personal and legal problems mounting, the president could attract defenders of the caliber of Gore Vidal, who spoke darkly about a backdoor revenge mounted by the insurance oligarchy through the third-party agency of Kenneth Starr. Perhaps encouraged by this, Clinton belatedly came out for a Patients' Bill of Rights, proposed by many in Congress to protect Americans from the depredations of HMOs. This last triangulation—offering to help plug a wound that he had himself inflicted—was perhaps the most satisfying of all. In a strong field, it remains perhaps the most salient example of the Clintonian style of populism for the poor and reassurance for the rich or, if you prefer, big pieces of pie for the fat cats and "good government" for the rest.

Whether the "capital" is moral or political or just plain financial, the Clinton practice is to use other peoples'. Some good judges would cite campaign financing, even more than health care, as the classic demonstration of that principle in operation. Perhaps more than any one thing, the system of private political fund-raising licenses the plaintive yelp, routinely emitted by anyone indicted or accused, to the effect that "everybody does it." Even by this debased standard, however, the Clinton administration was to achieve prodigies of innovation and excess. It was also to show ingenuity in the confection of excuses and alibis. One of these excuses was "privacy." No sooner had the suggestion been made that the Clintons were auctioning off the Lincoln Bedroom than Neil Lattimore, then the First Lady's press secretary, replied with indignation: "This is their home, and they have guests visit them all the time. Mrs. Clinton and Chelsea have friends that spend the night, but these names are not available to the public." The vulgar "public," which actually owns the White House, has no right to peek inside. Second-order stonewall replies took the more traditional form of the "security" defense, the separation of powers defense, and the flat-out lie. The Center for Public Integrity in Washington, which first tried to ventilate the matter, was told by the social secretary's office that: "No one in the White House will release that kind of information about guests anyway. I think it's for security reasons." The president's associate counsel, Marvin Krislov, discovered that "The Office of the President is not an 'agency' for purposes of the Freedom of

Information Act," a "finding" that was worth having for its own sake. And Amy Weiss Tobe, press secretary to the Democratic National Committee, said of the story: "This has become an urban myth, like the alligators in the sewers of New York. It is just not true."

There may be no carnivorous reptiles in the underground waterways of Manhattan, but it was eventually established that almost eighty major donors and fund-raisers had indeed been thrashing about in the Lincoln and the Queen's bedrooms at 1600 Pennsylvania Avenue. The invitations were sometimes offered as rewards, and sometimes as inducements. Steven Grossman, president of the Massachusetts Envelope Company and of the America-Israel Public Affairs Committee (AIPAC), contributed at least $400,000 to the Democratic party and to Mr. Clinton's election campaigns between 1991 and 1996. Nor was an overnight stay at the White House—following a state dinner for the president of Brazil—his only reward. His wife Barbara was appointed by the president to the National Council of the Arts, and he himself became a "managing trustee" for the Democratic National Committee. Other beneficiaries-cum-benefactors included David Geffen and Steven Spielberg of Dreamworks ($389,000 and $236,500, respectively), the Waltons of Wal-Mart ($216,800), the Nortons of Norton Utilities ($350,750), and Larry and Shelia Lawrence of the Hotel del Coronado and associated real estate ($100,000, counting contributions from their companies and their company's employees.) Despite the rumors about a liaison between the president and Mrs. Lawrence, the Clintons always insisted on high standards of propriety, stipulating for example that unmarried couples—even consenting ones— could not sleep together in Mr. Lincoln's chamber. Mr. Lawrence later achieved a brief celebrity by his triple crown of buying, lying, and dying: buying the ambassadorship to Switzerland, lying about his wartime service, and consequently being exhumed from Arlington Cemetery, where he had been mistakenly interred with full fund-raising honors.

The franchising of the Lincoln Bedroom gave way ultimately to the selling of the Oval Office itself. At forty-four separate "coffee" meetings between August 3, 1995 and August 23, 1996, President Clinton personally received the sweepings of the international black-bag community in his official quarters, and asked them for money. "Nice to see you again," he says to Roger Tamraz, pipeline artist and fugitive from justice, on one of the videos shot by the White House Communications Agency (WHCA). These videos became a source of controversy, for two reasons. During the Senate inquiry into the breach of campaign finance laws, in October 1997, the White House promised to turn over all materials relating to solicitation. The tapes, however, were not "discovered" by administration officials until the deadline was almost past. Then there was a further delay in handing them to the Justice Department. The legal deadline for Attorney General Reno to decide on whether or not to "expand" her inquiry was Friday, October 4. The tapes—the existence of which had been confirmed to Senate investigators the preceding Wednesday—were delivered to Justice on Saturday, October 5. No official explanation for this—at minimum—1,680-minute delay was ever offered by the White House.

The second reason for the brief notoriety of the tapes was the appearance on one of them of John Huang, a Chinese financier and fund-raiser with intimate connections in Beijing. He is shown shaking Clinton's hand on June 18, on the only tape which has no audio. Because the soundtrack was sadly missing, allegations from other witnesses that Mr. Huang opened the proceedings with a fund-raising appeal could not be confirmed. It is not legal to use the public-business spaces of the executive mansion—the Oval

Office, the Roosevelt Room, and the Map Room—for the shaking down of
the well-heeled, and most especially not for the shaking down of the well-
heeled emissaries of foreign despotisms in China, Indonesia, and the
Middle East. Donald L. Fowler, national co-chairman of the Democratic
party, shows a lively and acute awareness of this when, on a videotape from
the Map Room on December 13, 1995, he is heard declining an offer of five
checks from an unidentified guest as the president discusses golf. "As soon
as this thing is over, I'll call you," says Fowler, while making a suggestive
passing reference to the legal profession. "I'm sorry. I can't take this. I apol-
ogize to you, and we'll get it done." It got done, all right.

The pen of a Thomas Nast would be required to do justice to Lanny J.
Davis, a "special counsel" to the White House. "Holding this type of event
was legal and appropriate," he said on October 5, 1997. "There is no suggestion that there was any solicitation for money." On the same day he
added: "These tapes are not inconsistent with what we have previously
described to be the purpose of these coffees: to encourage people to support the President and his programs and that included financial support."
So checks were written but only after the event and were thus, he maintained, "incidental." As for keeping those innocuous tapes from the later
Senate inquiry: "That was inadvertent. We have always acted in good faith."
Several senators mentioned the ominous words "obstruction of justice."
(In late 1998, Mr. Davis's skills were required again to stave off impeach-
ment, and he returned from private practice to the White House team.
Shall I ever forget appearing with him on TV on the day of the impeach-
ment vote, and hearing him say that there was nothing Nixonian about
Clinton, before urging all good men and women to support the "censure"
compromise dreamed up by the Nixon-pardoning Gerald Ford?)

It may be worth noting that Mr. Clinton took federal matching funds from the taxpayers to keep pace with his exorbitant spending, and never pretended to be "out of the loop." One video of a high-tab feast at the Hay-Adams Hotel, on December 7, 1995, has him gloating to his contributors: "We realized we could run these ads through the Democratic party, which means we could raise [soft] money in twenty, fifty, and one-hundred thousand dollar blocks. We didn't have to do it all in thousand-dollar contributions and run down what I can spend, which is limited by law. So that is what we have done." A video of another Lucullan repast at this hotel, on February 19, 1996, has him thanking his benefactors in the same fulsome way: "In the last quarter of last year ... we spent about $1 million per week to advertise our point of view to somewhere between 26 and 42 percent of the American electorate ... The lead that I enjoy today in public opinion polls is about one-third due to that advertising ... I cannot overstate to you the impact that these paid ads have had." Since soft money is by definition not to be lawfully spent in promoting a candidate, Mr. Clinton appears to have been more unbuttoned and candid to his bankrollers than he ever was with the target voters. But that's populism for you. Dick Morris did not lie when he said that "Every line of every ad came under his informed, critical and often meddlesome gaze. Every ad was *his* ad." In other words, Clinton's the one.

So much so, as it happens, that somebody managed to move large sums of the soft money raised by the agile internationalist Charlie Trie, and transfer them from the coffers of the Democratic party to the account of the Clinton Legal Defense Fund. Here is the perfect paradox of public and private: where the Democrats are a public and accountable party dealing in deniable and surreptitious funds, while the president in his legal capacity is a private citizen subject to audit and disclosure. Even so, the two wires became inextricably crossed. That could have been embarrassing, if anyone had cared to make anything of it. Generally speaking, though, the Clinton forces have always been able to count upon Republican discretion—even understanding—when it comes to difficulties about political money.

For all that, the 4,878 pages of the report by the House Committee on Government Oversight may be reduced to one single sentence: "Because of the unprecedented lack of cooperation of witnesses, including 120 relevant individuals who either asserted Fifth Amendment privileges or fled the country, both the House and Senate investigations were severely hampered." By February 1999, this number had risen to 121. The Committee's indispensable report provides partial but illuminating accounts of covert donations by the Chinese military-industrial complex and its Indonesian surrogates, of favors returned to those who could produce brown bags of funny money (Charlie Trie was appointed to the Commission on U.S.–Pacific Trade and Investment Policy), and of mutual stroking between the Clinton administration and a number of foreign dictatorships. And it makes one thing piercingly clear. Those *one hundred and twenty one* potential witnesses who either left town or took the Fifth, who either "fled or pled," had as urgent a need as the President to assert their right to privacy.

On September 18, 1997, the Senate inquiry called Roger Tamraz, who revealed that he had paid $300,000 for his coffee at the White House and—showing the contempt which the "donor community" manifested throughout—added that next time he'd make it $600,000. Dick Morris was not called to testify, but did submit a 500-page deposition in which he proudly recalled his delight at finding a way through the legally imposed spending limits. By using "soft money" for "issue ads," and dumping a fortune into early TV spots, and by the not-unrelated tactic of stealing the Republicans' clothes (because big donors don't show up for campaign breakfasts to "keep welfare as we know it"), Morris was able to buy a commanding lead in the polls. Mr. Clinton evidently regarded Mr. Morris's covert control over policy, and his personal "cut" of the take amounting to almost $1.5 million, as a price well worth paying. I remember George Stephanopoulos ruefully reminiscing: "For eight months of 1995 and 1996, Morris was the president." And the scandal is not so much that nobody voted for Morris. It's the fact that, for much of that time, he operated under a Clinton-assigned code name and *nobody knew he was there.* By the time the stolen and bought and staged election was over, and the Democrats were hastily paying back the millions they had accepted from crepuscular overseas sources, the damage was done, and the entire electorate had been triangulated by a man whose only mistake was to be caught having illicit sex. (I allude, of course, to Mr. Morris.)

In the critical days of his impeachment struggle, Mr. Clinton was often said to be worried sick about his place in history. That place, however, is already secure. He will be remembered as the man who used the rhetoric of the New Democrat to undo the New Deal. He will also be remembered as a man who offered a groaning board of incentives for the rich and draconian admonitions to the poor.

The centerpiece of his legacy was "welfare reform." The passage of a timely pre-election bill, removing federal guarantees from impoverished children for the first time in sixty years, became essential not only to President Morris but to President Clinton as well. Not only did it annex the main "issue" from the Republicans, it also provided background and depth to the unending Clintonian homilies about moral continence, thrift, and family values. It signaled, to approving audiences among the better fed, that for the indigent, "the party was over." The many who had never been invited to this supposed party were less inclined to vote, and less able to register. And the children among them, of course, did not vote at all. Nor were their opinions solicited by Mr. Morris's expensive pollsters.

As Peter Edelman, the most dedicated and expert worker in the field of welfare and family, pointed out to me:

> There is a submerged class question here. I always get at it in my speeches by pointing out the hypocrisy in the rhetoric as to who should stay at home with their children. Many on the right (and elsewhere) are saying mothers should stay at home with their small children because the new research data on brain development shows that small children need that stimulation. These same people then turn around and say poor moms have to go out and work immediately. (Many states have work requirements beginning when an infant is twelve weeks old, and the vast majority of the remainder require work when the child is a year old.) That's a pretty clear class distinction.

But, as we are endlessly instructed, while rich people will *not* work unless they are given money, poor people will *only* work if they are not. (These are the two modern meanings of the term "incentive": a tax break on the one hand and the threat of the workhouse on the other.) And, once the Democratic party had adopted this theology, the poor had no one to whom they could turn. The immediate consequence of this was probably an intended one: the creation of a large helot underclass disciplined by fear and scarcity, subject to endless surveillance, and used as a weapon against any American worker lucky enough to hold a steady or unionized job.

The evidence lies all around us, and will be around us for some time to come. Whether it is gleaned from the most evenhanded and "responsible" reporting, such as that of Jason DeParle atop the great rampart of the *New York Times*, or from writers like Christopher Cook in the *Progressive*, we shall have to accustom ourselves to stories like this. In Missouri, under the Direct Job Placement scheme (such schemes are always known officially as "initiatives"), the state bureaucracy mutates itself into a hiring hall for cheap labor in junk-nutrition conglomerates such as Tyson Foods. Welfare recipients are told to sign on and gut fifty chickens a minute, or be wiped from the rolls of the new Poor Law. They are directed to an industry which is well used to turnover among employees:

> As one woman on welfare discovered [never mind her name], even having a newborn baby and no means of transportation is no excuse. When the thirty-year-old mother informed her case managers of these extenuating circumstances, they were not sympathetic. "They told her she had to work at Tyson's even if she had to walk to get there—a six-mile trek," says Helen Chewning, a former family advocate with the Missouri Valley Human Resource Center in Sedalia. "They sanctioned her while she was pregnant," and then ordered her to work at Tyson's when her baby was just eleven days old. She hasn't had any income for six months. How are they supposed to live?"

The process of "sanctioning"—the new state euphemism for coercion via the threat of cut-off—involves facing defenseless people with the rather old choice between "work or starve." It is the tactic by which welfare rolls are being "trimmed," if you will allow another Clintonian euphemism. You can be "sanctioned" if you refuse any job, or miss any interview.

I did not select Missouri because it's a famously unsentimental state. I selected it because President Clinton, in an August 1997 address to businessmen in St. Louis, touted it as the model laboratory for his welfare reform. It's useful only for dialectical purposes to mention that Tyson Foods uses the Direct Job Placement scheme as its taxpayer-funded recruiting sergeant. The first shock of recognition, experienced by those who are supposed to be grateful for a dose of nonalienated and dignified labor, is the "puller job." This involves gutting birds—later to provide tasteless nourishment at the tables of the badly off—at a rapid rate. The fingernails of the inexperienced are likely to be the first to go; dissolved in bacteria and chicken fat. Of Missouri's 103,000 poultry workers, according to the Bureau of Labor Statistics, almost one-third endured an injury or an illness in 1995 alone. That this may be an undercounting is suggested by the experience of one hard-pressed toiler on the Tyson chicken-thigh assembly line named Jason Wolfe: "They want you to hang forty or fifty of these birds in a minute, for four to six hours straight, without a break. If you miss any, they threaten to fire you." He himself was fired because of too many "sick days."

Supplied by the state with a fearful, docile labor force, the workhouse masters are relatively untroubled by unions, or by any back-talk from the staff. Those who have been thus "trimmed" from the welfare rolls have often done no more than disappear into a twilight zone of casual employment, uninsured illness, intermittent education for their children, and unsafe or temporary accommodation. Only thus—by their disappearance from society—can they be counted as a "success story" by ambitious governors, and used in order to qualify tightfisted states for "caseload-reduction credits" from the federal government. The women among them, not infrequently pressed for sexual favors as the price of the ticket, can be asked at random about the number of toothbrushes found in the trailer, and are required by law to name the overnight guest or the father of the child if asked. Failure or refusal to name the father can lead to termination of "benefits" or (an even better word) "entitlements." We were once told from the bought-and-sold Oval Office itself, that "even presidents are entitled to privacy": it seems now that *only* presidents and their wealthy backers can claim this entitlement. I pause again to note that Tyson Foods, which is based in Arkansas, has spread a banquet of donations before Bill Clinton ever since his boyhood as a candidate, and that its famously colorful chairman Don Tyson sits in a corporate sanctum modeled to scale on the Oval Office itself, with the doorknobs shaped in ovals to resemble chicken eggs. Truly was it said that the poor have such people always with them.

In the great city and state of New York, once the redoubt of Democratic liberalism, a federal audit in January 1999 found that "city officials routinely violate the law by denying poor people the right to apply promptly for food stamps, fail to screen families for emergency food needs, require the poor to search for jobs before receiving help, and cut off food stamps to needy families who were still eligible for those benefits." As for those who had—in Mayor Giuliani's boastful words—"left" the welfare rolls for gainful employment, a state survey of those dropped between July 1996 and March 1997 found that only 29 percent of those dismissed from welfare had found employment—"employment" being defined as earning $100 over three months. Many of the rest, as in even more exacting states like Wisconsin, had simply gone missing. So had their children, because as already noted children don't vote while—as nobody understands better than Clinton—retired people do. These vanished Americans had merged into a ballooning underclass which is not even head-counted in the age of cheerful statistics, and which will show up only on the other side of the shining span of bridge that beckoned us to the 21st century.

Should all else fail, the poor of Missouri or any other of the fifty states could enlist in the employer of last resort, the military, where they could be subjected at random to mandatory drug tests (which are well on their way to becoming a craze in private industry as well) and legally prohibited from committing adultery. Should their personal tastes have ripened to warmth in the embrace of their own gender, they could be hounded and prosecuted by the Navy Investigative Service or its equivalent. If they were ostensibly male and wed and heterosexual and even suspected of deviance, their wives could also be visited without warning by the NIS and asked such leading questions as: "Did he ever fuck you up the ass?" (This question and others like it were documented by the late Randy Shilts, a real hero among the chroniclers of gay history and experience.) Failure to cooperate, or to incriminate others, could lead at once to unemployment or to disgrace—or both at once—and, in not a few cases, to incarceration. Such persecutions markedly increased during the Clinton era, with discharges for sexual incorrectness touching an all-time high in 1998. Mr. Clinton can also claim credit for warrantless searches of public housing and the innovation of the "roving wiretap." If any successor to Arthur Miller wanted to depict a modern Salem, he would do better to investigate the hysteria of the war on drugs, where to be suspected is to be guilty. In 1995, arrests for drug offenses that involved no violence were numbered at 1.5 million per annum, having climbed 31 percent in Mr. Clinton's first three years of tenure. The crime and terrorism statutes enacted in the same period caused even his most dogmatic apologists—Anthony Lewis, most notably—to wince.

An early and demagogic adoption of mandatory sentences, of the moronic chant of "three strikes and you're out," and of the need for speedy capital sentences was, of course, part of the Dick Morris strategy.

But it was also an element in Clinton's attempt to distance himself from the bleeding hearts of the Democratic party and to recast himself as a Southern sheriff. As a direct and intended result of this make-over, minors and the mentally ill are arraigned for the death penalty in America, the appeals procedure from Death Row has been abruptly and arbitrarily curtailed, and there is an execution every five days. The protection of habeas corpus has been withdrawn from immigrants, life sentences may be mandated for stunned defendants and imposed by shocked judges for the possession of cannabis alone, and sentences for possession of "crack" cocaine, a poor people's drug, are ten times harsher than those for possession of the powder cocaine consumed by the rich. The prison economy outperforms the college economy even in states like California, and the incarceration rate for American citizens is many multiples higher that of any European nation, and barely trails behind that of Russia.

By 1997, all economic analysts were showing an abrupt and widening gap in income distribution in the United States, with many more super-rich and many more abjectly poor, and an astonishing increase in the number of "working poor" who, even with tough and unrewarding jobs, are unable to earn enough to transcend officially defined poverty. (Income distribution is often compared by classical economists to a diamond-diagram, with an upper and lower apex and a thinner or fatter middle. A diamond diagram, of course, is two triangles piled on top of one another.) In softer and apparently less coercive tones, meanwhile, the First Lady appeared on platforms to tell people what was in their own best interests, and to demand a tobacco-free and "buckle-up" society as well. For millions of people living in the Clinton epoch, "the era of big government" was by no means "over." It had, in fact, just begun.

All of the above had to be endured, in order that gay and feminist and civil rights and civil libertarian forces could "come together" in the midterm elections of November 1998, and exclaim almost with one voice that racism and oligarchy threatened their president and his spouse, and that government should be kept out of the bedroom.

A single expression, culled from that bizarre period and kept (at least by this reviewer) like a fragrant petal pressed between the leaves of an old and cherished book, will do duty for the entire period of hysterical illusion. I shall preserve it lovingly, until long after those who uttered it have pretended with embarrassment that they never did. That expression is "the coup." Which Clintonoid columnist or propagandist did not employ this dramatic phrase, as their hero found himself at the mercy, not of a law 'n' order Democrat on the approved model, but of a law 'n' order Republican? (The most the Republican leadership could have hoped to achieve was the confirmation of Al Gore as President two years before his time—some coup.) The term *coup* refers, properly as well as metaphorically, to an abrupt seizure of power by unelected forces, along the lines of the *pronunciamenti* so well remembered by our southern neighbors. It is sometimes given its full dignity in French as *coup d'état*, or "blow at the state," and was in that form employed by many of the outraged Democrats who took the floor of the House on December 19, 1998. Their outrage was directed not at any action of their commander in chief but at any motion to depose him or even to impugn his character.

On that day, Clinton ordered the smiting of Mesopotamia. At the time, this decision seemed to complete his adoption of the military-industrial worldview, though in fact his full and absolute conversion to that theology lay two weeks ahead. One may also find the origins of his conversion in his past. Clinton's relationship with the unelected and unaccountable uniformed para-state is, in some ways, an old story. It is known that he opposed the war on Vietnam, and it is also known that he dodged, rather than resisted, the draft. The distinction is not without a difference. Looking back, George Stephanopoulos shudders to recall the moment in 1992 when a reporter handed him a Xeroxed copy of Clinton's draft notice. This, after candidate Clinton assured him that no such summons had ever been issued, and instructed him to say as much. It was later to emerge that candidate Clinton believed that all known copies of the document had been weeded from the files. In other words, Clinton borrowed the moral prestige of the antiwar movement in order to shield his own skin.

I myself recall reading with keen interest Clinton's 1969 letter to his draft board when news of it broke. Obviously wasted on the colonel to whom it was addressed, it breathes with much of the spirit of those most defensible of days. Clinton had written of "working everyday with a depth of feeling I had reserved solely for racism in America before Vietnam." And he had protested having to "fight and kill and die" in such a war, with the verbs not only in the morally correct order but repeated as "fight, kill and maybe die" lower down. Anyone who believes that the objection of antiwar activists was to personal danger rather than to complicity in atrocity and aggression just wasn't there at the time. Also redolent of the period was Clinton writing in the same letter, "I decided to accept the draft in spite of my beliefs for one reason: to maintain my political viability within the system." "Within the system" is vintage 1960s, but now I wonder. Who else of that band of brave and cheerful young Americans, so apparently selfless in their opposition to their country's disgrace, was asking, "How will this play in New

Hampshire in around 1992?" The thought gave me the creeps, though perhaps it shouldn't have. Someone had to be thinking about the long haul, I suppose. But I would bet a goodly sum that most of those concerned were not planning much beyond the downfall of Richard Nixon. A calculating young man this Clinton, in any event.

Once elected, he never even pretended that civilian control was the operative principle. Harry Truman, no friend of the white feather or the conscientious objector, fired General Douglas MacArthur without overmuch hesitation when he challenged presidential authority, and withstood the subsequent opinion-poll and populist riot, and probably lost no more shut-eye than he did when incinerating Hiroshima and Nagasaki. ("New Democrats" in that epoch knew how to be tough.) Bill Clinton was no sooner elected than, bullied by the Joint Chiefs, he broke his election promise to open the ranks to gays. He then allowed Colin Powell, the hero of Panama and My Lai, to dictate a policy of capitulation to the junta in Haiti and the national socialists in Belgrade. And he catered faithfully to military-industrial constituencies, supporting exorbitant weapons-building projects like the Seawolf submarine, in which even the Pentagon had lost interest. No matter how fanciful or budget-busting the concept, from the B-1 bomber upwards, Clinton always relaxed his commitment to trimming government spending and invariably advocated not only a welfare "safety net" for the likes of General Dynamics and Boeing, but a handout free and clear.

This had been standard practice among Democratic aspirants during the haunted years of the contest with Soviet Russia, where "softness" was at an understandable discount among sophisticated and ambitious liberals. However, Mr. Clinton was the first postwar and post–Cold War president. His "watch" occurred during a unique and unprecedented period of military and political relaxation, when the totalitarian codes of "launch on warning" and "balance of terror" had been abandoned even by many of their former advocates. Let the record show, then, that the Clinton White House took no step of any kind to acknowledge, much less take advantage of this new reality, and always acted as if the most paranoid predictions of John Foster Dulles were about to be fulfilled. With the help of a tremendous lobbying effort from the aerospace and other defense conglomerates, the NATO alliance was "enlarged," at least partly to furnish a sales market for those in "the contractor community" who would otherwise have had to close production lines. The budget of the Central Intelligence Agency was increased, while democratic "oversight" of its activity was held to a myopic level and even the records of its past activities in Guatemala, Chile, and Iran were shrouded or shredded (illegally at that) without demur. The Clinton administration contrived the feat of being the only major government in the West to make no comment on the arrest of General Pinochet, despite the existence of outstanding cases of American citizens murdered on his direct instructions. The promiscuous sale of arms and technology to other countries, including existing dictatorships as well as potential ones, was enthusiastically pursued. Not an eyebrow was raised when the "special forces" of the Indonesian army, trained and equipped for the sole purpose of combating malcontent Indonesian civilians, were found to have been supervised by United States authorities in open defiance of a supposed congressional ban.

Conducting relations with the bankrupt and humiliated "former superpower," Clinton and his understrappers Strobe Talbott and Sandy Berger followed a policy which history may well remember, of always covering up for their diseased autocratic marionette Boris Yeltsin when he was wrong (in Chechnya and in Bosnia and in Mafia matters) and always weakening him when he was in the right (as in their breaches of promise about the expansion of NATO and the demolition of the ABM treaty). No doubt they considered his bleary, raging, oafish conduct to be a "private" issue, kept as it was from being investigated by any legal authority in the new Russia.

In a manner which actually mirrors rather than contradicts the above, Bill Clinton sometimes did find the strength and the nerve to disagree with his military chiefs. He overruled them when they expressed doubts on the rocketing of Khartoum and Afghanistan in August 1998. But on that occasion, he had urgent political reasons of his own to wish to "stand tall." All was made whole on January 6, 1999, when the president announced, even as the Senate was convening on his impeachment, that the dearest wish of the Joint Chiefs and the Republican Right would be granted after all. After twenty years and $55 billion spent on a series of completely unsuccessful "tests," he promised that an actual $7 billion would be set aside to build a "Star Wars" missile system. The figure, much understated, was in a sense irrelevant, because the promise to "build," rather than to experiment, was the threshold which neither Reagan nor Bush had crossed. But Clinton claimed, in his State of the Union address in January 1999, that there had been a terrible shortfall in military expenditure since the middle of 1985—high noon of the Reagan era. Triangulation could go no further.

A September report in the *New York Times* completes the picture. Leaked by someone close to the Joint Chiefs, it shows the president—a king of shreds and patches—summoned to a uniformed conclave at the National Defense University in Fort McNair and there informed that he has lost his moral standing as commander in chief, because laws enforceable on officers and other ranks have been flouted by himself. Within weeks, he was proffering a hitherto unbudgeted increase in military spending of $110 billion over six years—another boost to big government for the rich and another reminder of good government for the poor. Along with the mooted handover of Social Security funds to Wall Street, this was the fabled "agenda" from which, according to solemn Democratic commentators, the country was being distracted by a distressing focus on the president's personal crookery. The cover-up and the "agenda," however, soon became indistinguishable as Clinton played out the bipartisan hand to the end.

In the Clinton administration's relationship with the international community, the policy of triangulation almost satirizes itself. Thanks to an unusually warm and fetid relationship between Senator Jesse Helms on the one hand—he being chairman of the Senate Foreign Relations Committee—and Ms. Madeleine Albright on the other, the Clinton administration was and is the only important negative vote on the establishment of a land mines treaty, and on the setting up of an international body to try war criminals. (The other noteworthy "contras" are Saddam Hussein's Iraq and Colonel Qaddafi's Libya.) The same administration also uses the UN as a ditto for U.S. unilateralism, all the time contemptuously refusing to pay its dues to the world body.

"Globalization," usually the company song of the American corporate strategy, stops at the water's edge and turns prickly and isolationist when it comes to the rights of others to judge American actions. This dualism was seen to perfect effect when Clinton supported the Jesse Helms and Dan Burton legislation, which not merely intensified the stupid embargo on Cuba but presumptuously extended it into an attack on trade with Havana conducted by third countries like Canada, France, or Great

Britain. This covert understanding is arrived at by means of a sweetheart deal with Dick Morris's former boss in North Carolina.

Over the course of seven precious and irrecoverable years of potential peace and disarmament, then, Clinton has squandered every conceivable opportunity for a renegotiated world order. He has been the front-man for a silent coup rather than the victim of one, and has learned, for a bad combination of private and public motives, to stop worrying and to love all bombs.

FOUR

A QUESTION OF CHARACTER

AT THE INITIAL moment of the Clinton campaign in 1992, there was much pompous talk about the question of "character." This was relatively easily deflected by those who maintained, and also by those who were paid to maintain, that "issues" should weigh more than "personalities." And, at that same initial moment, the line that favored issues over personalities seemed to many people the more serious one—the one for the high-minded to take. One can still hear this echo, like the last squeak from a dying planet, in the automatic response of those poll respondents and other loyalists who say that they care more about health insurance than about Monica Lewinsky.

Well, I could sign my own name to *that* proposition. But could Clinton? And wasn't that the point to begin with? In 1992, it seemed to many people that the late Paul Tsongas, a man of probity and competence and fiscal integrity, was the authentic "New Democrat." A bit bloodless perhaps, and a bit low on compassion, but an efficient technocrat and a modernizer. Mr. Clinton had nothing substantial to put against Tsongas's program. He just thought that he, and not Mr. Tsongas, should be the nominee and the one who enjoyed the fruits of office. So "personality" came into it from the start, and all denials of that fact are idle. Not one—I repeat, not one—of Clinton's team in 1992 did not harbor the fear that a "flaw" might embarrass and even humiliate everybody. Was this not a recognition of the character issue, however oblique? Some thought it would be funny money, some thought it would be "bimbo eruptions," a few guessed that it would be a sordid combination of the two. All were prepared to gloss it over in favor of the big picture, of getting the job done, or of getting a job for themselves.

The Establishment injunction—to focus on "issues" and "concerns" and "agendas" rather than mere "personalities"—is overripe for the garbage heap. The whole apparatus of professionalized and privatized political management is devoted to the idea of "the candidate," and it is to a person with a memory for names and faces, rather than to any computer-generated manifesto, that donors at home and abroad give large sums of money that the newspapers don't discover until it's too late. Moreover, the judgment of "character" is one of the few remaining decisions that an otherwise powerless and unconsulted voter is able to make for himself (or, and here I defer to Ann Lewis, for herself). Simply put, a candidate can change his/her campaign platform when in office, but he/she cannot change his/her nature. Even more simply put, the honest and the powerless have a vested interest in a politician who cannot be bought, whereas the powerful and the dishonest have already begun to haggle over the tab while the acceptance speech is still being written. And, even in a political system renowned worldwide for its venality, Bill Clinton seemed anxious to be bought, and willing if not indeed eager to advertise the fact in advance.

Venturing, then, onto the territory of sociopathy, one can notice some other filiations between the public and private Clinton. There is, clearly, something very distraught in his family background. Our physicians tell us that that thirst for approval is often the outcome of a lonely or insecure childhood (and Clinton's entire menu of initiatives, from provincial governor to provincial president, betrays a preoccupation with the small and wheedling and ingratiating effect), but what about this, from Hillary Clinton's book *It Takes a Village*? In 1986, Chelsea Clinton was six:

> One night at the dinner table, I told her, "You know, Daddy is going to run for governor again. If he wins, we would keep living in this house, and he would keep trying to help people. But first we have to have an election. And that means other people will try and convince voters to vote for them instead of for Daddy. One of the ways they may do this is by saying terrible things about him." Chelsea's eyes went wide, and she asked, "What do you mean?" We explained that in election campaigns, people might even tell lies about her father in order to win, and we wanted her to be ready for that. Like most parents, we had taught her that it was wrong to lie, and she struggled with the idea, saying over and over, "Why would people do that?" I didn't have an answer for that one. (I still don't.) Instead, we asked her to pretend she was her dad and was making a speech about why people should vote for her. She said something like, "I'm Bill Clinton. I've done a good job and I've helped a lot of people. Please vote for me." We praised her and explained that now her daddy was going to pretend to be one of the men running against

him. So Bill said terrible things about himself, like how he was really mean to people and didn't try to help them. Chelsea got tears in her eyes and said, "Why would anybody say things like that?"

According to the First Lady, it took several repeats of this "role-playing" exercise before the kid stopped crying. Heaven knows what things are like now, with the daddy president having used the same child as a prop to gull the public between January and August 1998. He's not much better with the more mature females, either. Mr. Clinton held precisely two Cabinet meetings—count them—in 1998. At the first one, immediately after the first Lewinsky revelation in January, he convened his team and asked them to step outside in the street and echo his falsehoods, which many of them did. At the second one, in August, he told them that he was moving to Plan B, and telling some part of the truth. Donna Shalala thereupon asked him if he had not, perhaps, put his own interests above those of his colleagues and even—heaven forbid—his agenda. At once, and according to eyewitnesses, the supposedly contrite chief executive whirled upon her. "If it was up to you, Nixon would have been better than Kennedy in 1960." There was a craven silence in the room—anyone who had lasted that long with Clinton must already have had a self-respect deficit that a lifetime won't requite—but afterwards someone was heard to murmur thoughtfully: "He'll say *anything.*"

I have known a number of people who work for and with, or who worked for and with, this man. They act like cult members while they are still under the spell, and talk like ex–cult members as soon as they have broken away. Even the disgraced Webster Hubbell, whose loyalty to Clinton is based on cronyism and on the old requirement of knowing what to do for the boss without having to be told, has had his moments of anxiety. Promoted from the revolving-door back-slappery of the Arkansas "business community" to the halls of the Justice Department, he was taken to one side by the new president and "tasked" with two occult inquiries. "Find out who killed Kennedy, and tell me whether there are UFOs or not." At other moments, staff have been asked to Camp David to meet with "enablers" and other shamans of the New Age. The vacuous language of uplift and therapy, commingled with the tawdry pieties of Baptist and Methodist hypocrisy, clings to both Clintons like B.O. It was suggested by the First Lady herself that her husband's off-the-record meetings with a female intern were a form of "ministry."

This obtuse righteousness is inscribed in every move, physical or political, that the Clintons make. Neither ever offers—for all their tin-roof "humility"—a word of self-criticism. The president has been told for many years, by advisors who in some cases adore him, that he must not speak for too long when given the podium. His prolixity remains stubborn and incurable, yet it remains a fact that in all his decades of logorrhea Clinton has failed to make a single remark (absent some lame catch phrases like "New Covenant" and of course the imperishable "It all depends on what the meaning of 'is' is") that could possibly adhere to the cortex of a thinking human being. The Oval Office may have presented itself to him as a potentially therapeutic location, but once he arrived there he half realized that he had no big plans, no grand thoughts, no noble dreams. He also realized that he might have to give up one of the few things that did bring him release from his demons. He lost little time in substituting the one for the other, and reacted with extreme indignation when confronted with the disclosure of the fact. This was the empty rage of Caliban glimpsing his visage in the glass. It was not the first such instance, or even the most revealing. The driveling idiom of therapy was his only alternative to red-faced self-righteousness, as when he was interviewed in September 1998:

> You know some people say to me, "I feel so terrible for you. It's been so awful what has been publicized to the whole country; the whole world." Believe it or not, and I know it's hard for people to believe, that has not bothered me very much because of the opportunity I've had to seek spiritual counseling and advice and to think through this and to try to focus much more on how I can properly atone, how I can be forgiven, and then how I can go back to healing with my family.

A month later he was to describe his short-lived public-relations triumph at the disastrous Wye agreement with Benjamin Netanyahu and Yasir Arafat, as a step on his own "path of atonement." And two months after that, it was bombs away again over Baghdad. Mrs. Ceausescu must have had days of ministry like this.

As early as April 1993, according to an eyewitness account given to Bob Woodward for his book *The Agenda*, Clinton found himself with nothing to propose, and nothing to give away. He had been told that the bond market and its managers had boxed him in. He lost his temper to an operatic degree. "I hope you're all aware we're all Eisenhower Republicans," he bellowed to his team. "We're Eisenhower Republicans here, and we are fighting with Reagan Republicans. We stand for lower deficits and free trade and the bond market. Isn't that great? . . . We must have something for the common man. It won't hurt me in 1994, and I can put enough into '95 and '96 to crawl through to reelection. At least we'll have health care to give them, if we can't give them anything else."

I cannot guess what it's like for a Democratic loyalist to read that bombast now. The Republicanism of Clinton's presidency has not, in fact, risen to the Eisenhower level. He has entrusted policy to much more extreme Republicans like Alan Greenspan and Dick Morris, without manifesting any of the old general's robust suspicion of the military-industrial complex. (And it's impossible to imagine Eisenhower, who always showed contempt for his venal vice-president, making the spectacle of himself that Clinton made at Nixon's graveside.)

In 1996 I wrote an attack on the "lesser evil" theory of political choice, which was printed in *Dissent* magazine and discussed at its editorial board. There the editor, Michael Walzer, inquired plaintively: "Why is it that some people on the Left seem to *hate* Bill Clinton?" I thought then, and I think even more now, that the mystery lies elsewhere. Why do so many people on the *Right* hate Bill Clinton?

Of course, there's an element of the stupid party involved: the conservatives thought Franklin Roosevelt was a communist even as he saved capital from itself by means of the National Recovery Act. But Bill Clinton, who has gone further than Reagan ever dared in repealing the New Deal and seconding the social Darwinist ethic at home and abroad, is nonetheless detested on the Right. The old slogan, "draft-dodging, pot-smoking, lying, womanizing sonofabitch" still resonates. As why should it not, given that a person of such qualities has been able to annex and even anticipate the Republican platform, thereby demonstrating conclusively that there is no sufficient or necessary connection between the said platform and personal honor, or political honesty? At least Trent Lott and Newt Gingrich and the Christian Coalition got something for their frustration: the sight of Bomber Bill carrying a large Bible from prayer breakfast to prayer breakfast while ordering the downtrodden to shape up, and the war planes to discipline the wogs, and the military production lines to restart.

Walzer's question, at least in its inverted form, remains. It's become tiring to hear people on the Left say that Clinton should perhaps be arraigned, but not for anything he's actually been charged with. A vast number of liberal academics and intellectuals wouldn't even go that far, preferring to place themselves under the leadership of Arthur Schlesinger, Jr., as he instructed the Congress that a gentleman was obliged to lie, under any duress, in matters of sex. (Also that: "Only a cad tells the truth about his love affairs.") This polka-dotted popinjay has been himself permitted to lie, these many years, about the record of the Kennedy gang. But not until now had he been called as a witness on who is, or is not, a gentleman, let alone about what is, or is not, a "love affair." (On caddishness he perhaps does possess real historical expertise that was, alas, not sought by the House Judiciary Committee.) His nominee for the title of gentleman, however, was certainly in keeping with the standards he has upheld until now. Gentlemen are indeed supposed to be discreet about affairs, at any hazard to themselves, in order to protect the honor and modesty of the ladies involved. This doesn't quite track with Clinton's policy of maintaining a semi-official staff for the defamation and bullying of inconvenient but truthful former girlfriends: "the politics of personal destruction" elevated into an annex of the state machine. It is not "philandering"—a term of some dash and gaiety that has been much abused—to hit on the help and then threaten dire reprisals. A gentleman, having once implied that Gennifer Flowers was a lying gold digger, does not make it up to her, or to those he misled, by agreeing in a surly manner years later that perhaps he did sleep with her "once." All other considerations to one side, doesn't he know that it's the height of bad manners to make love to somebody only once? Those who claim to detect, in the widespread loathing of Clinton, an aggressive "culture war" against the freedom-loving sixties should be forced to ask themselves if Clinton, with his almost sexless conquests and his eerie affectless claim that the female felt no pleasure, represents the erotic freedom that they had in mind. (After the Juanita Broaddrick revelations, Schlesinger was not given the opportunity to say that a gentleman is obliged, if only from gallantry, to lie about rape.)

There remains the irony of Amendments 413 and 415 of Clinton's own crime bill, signed into law in September 1994, which permit a defendant in a sexual harassment lawsuit to be asked under oath about his other sexual entanglements. Lobbied by certain feminists for the inclusion of these amendments, Clinton had professed himself shocked that such a law was not already on the books. Thus when caught in his own law, and required by a Supreme Court vote of 9–0 to answer the questions, Clinton would commit various common law crimes if he decided to do other than tell the truth, let alone if he decided to recruit subordinates to lie. He would also be committing a crime that it is only in his power to commit—a direct violation of the presidential oath of office.

Gore Vidal was perhaps more honest than Schlesinger, and certainly more accurate, when he explained that: "Boys are meant to squirt as often as possible with as many different partners as possible. Girls are designed to take nine months to lay an egg ... Clinton doesn't much care for Warm Mature Relationships with Warm Caring Women. Hence an addiction to the impersonal blowjob." When he wrote this, Mr. Vidal was emerging as a defender of the president and a friend of the First Lady. I echo the desire of my friend Geoffrey Wheatcroft to see Hillary Clinton sitting next to Vidal "nodding gravely while he says that."

Is it not in fact rather clear that Clinton's conduct in the Lewinsky and Jones and Willey cases represents a microcosm of Clintonism itself? There is, first and most saliently, the use of public office for private ends and gratification. The bodyguards bring the chick to the room, just as in any banana republic, and the witnesses can be taken care of in the usual way, and the man who later uses the Lincoln Bedroom as an off-the-record rental for fat cats thinks nothing of claiming the Oval Office as a *chambre particulier.* There is, again, the fact that Monica Lewinsky was originally supplied to the White House on the recommendation of Walter Kaye, a bored and wealthy nonentity who later testified that he could not remember how much he had donated to Clintonian funds. (The relationship between the Kathleen Willey cover-up and Nathan Landow makes a similar point in a slightly different way.) There is, in a recurring pattern, the use of that other fund-raiser and influence-peddler Vernon Jordan to arrange soft landings and "deniability." There is, very conspicuously, the automatic resort to the use of publicly paid officials (some with their consent but most without) as liars and hacks for a supposedly "private and personal" matter. And where they fail, lawyers from the school of Cochrane and Dershowitz—loophole artists for rich thugs—are flung into the breach. Scarcely worth noticing, as being too predictable for words, is the employment of White House full-timers to spread the idea that Ms. Lewinsky was "a stalker"—as if a president, who surrounded the executive mansion with ugly concrete barriers out of concern for his personal safety, and who is protected night and day by men who are paid to take a bullet for him, could be unsafe from harassment in his "own" Oval Office.

Most telling, in a way, was the smearing of Ms. Jones as a woman so common and dirty that she might even have enjoyed an encounter with Clinton or, depending on which cover story was which, might have been actuated by the sort of greed only found in trailer parks. Here is the real contempt with which Clinton and his circle view the gullible rubes who make up their voting base: "those people whose toil and sweat sends us here and pays our way," as Clinton oleaginously phrased it in his banal first inaugural address. Since

that speech, he has never voluntarily spent any time in the company of anyone who earns money rather than makes it. And, when told by the United
States Supreme Court that he had to answer questions from an apparent
female nobody, under the terms of a statute on sexual harassment that he had
himself caused to be made law, he decided that he could lie his way out as he
always had. It's not much of a riposte, at this point, for Clinton's people to say
that the unfashionable nobody had some shady right-wing friends. However
shady they were, they didn't fall to the standard of Dick Morris.

When I look out of my window in Washington D.C., I am forced to confront the statue of General McClellan, which stands isolated in traffic at the
confluence of Connecticut Avenue and Columbia Road. The worst commander on either side in the Civil War, he was rightly suspected of surreptitious pro-slavery political ambitions and indeed ran against Lincoln as a
Democrat for the Presidency. His equestrian figure, whether by accident or
design, still has him pointing his horse away from the enemy and toward
the White House. Accepting the Democratic party's nomination on July 16,
1992, Clinton made the most of his Dixie drawl as he said: "I know how
President Lincoln felt when General McClellan wouldn't attack in the Civil
War. He asked him, 'If you're not going to use your army, may I borrow it?'
And so I say: George Bush, if you won't use your power to help people, step
aside. I will."

Karl Marx predicted McClellan's firing by Lincoln, and accused the
supposedly timorous general of an ill-concealed sympathy for the other
side. In demanding that Bush hand him the reins, Clinton pretended that
government would and should still be "activist" for the powerless. But he
was, in fact, a stealthy envoy from the enemy camp. In power, he has completed the Reagan counter-revolution and made the state into a personal
friend of those who are already rich and secure. He has used his armed

forces in fits of pique, chiefly against the far-off and the unpopular, and on dates which suit his own court calendar. The draft-dodger has mutated into a pliant serf of the Pentagon, the pot smoker into the chief inquisitor in the "war on drugs," and the womanizer into a boss who uses subordinates as masturbatory dolls. But the liar and the sonofabitch remain, and who will say that these qualities played no part in the mutation?

FIVE

CLINTON'S WAR CRIMES

TOWARD THE END of the amputated and perfunctory impeachment process, a small bleat was set up on the Internet and in the pages of America's half-dead left and liberal press. "Impeach President Clinton," said the appeal, "But For the Right Reasons." The signatories had noticed that Clinton used unbridled executive power to make war in what used to be called the Third World. But they thought that this ought to be sharply distinguished from his other promiscuities.

Reality, however, did not admit of any such distinction. In this instance, perhaps more than any other, Clinton's private vileness meshed exactly with his brutal and opportunistic public style. In idle moments, I used to amuse myself with the defining slogan of the herbivorous Left: "Think globally, act locally." It always seemed to me just as persuasive, and just about as inspiring, if phrased the other way around. How satisfying, then, that when Clinton acted globally, and did so for the most "localized" and provincial motives, it should have been the Left who were the last to see it.

This essay of mine, slightly adapted from its original form, appeared in *Vanity Fair* just as the predetermined vote on impeachment was coming up in the Senate. It shows the failure of all political forces to examine the most crucial, and the least scrutinized, of the failed counts of impeachment. That count is Abuse of Power.

*   *   *

This is an essay about canines. It concerns, first, the president of the United States and commander in chief of the U.S. armed forces, whose character was once memorably caught by a commentator in his native Arkansas who called him "a hard dog to keep on the porch." It concerns, second, the dog or dogs which did not bark in the nighttime. (In the Sherlock Holmes tale "Silver Blaze," the failure of such a beast to give tongue—you should pardon the expression—was the giveaway that exposed his master as the intruder.) And it concerns, third, the most famous dog of 1998: the dog that was wagged by its own tail. Finally, it concerns the dogs of war, and the circumstances of their unleashing.

Not once but three times last year, Bill Clinton ordered the use of cruise missiles against remote and unpopular countries. On each occasion, the dispatch of the missiles coincided with bad moments in the calendar of his long and unsuccessful struggle to avoid impeachment. Just before the Lewinsky affair became public in January 1998, there was a New York prescreening party for Barry Levinson's movie *Wag the Dog*, written by Hilary Henkin and

David Mamet. By depicting a phony president starting a phony war in order to distract attention from his filthy lunge at a beret-wearing cupcake, this film became the political and celluloid equivalent of a Clintonian roman à clef. Thrown by Jane Rosenthal and Robert DeNiro, whose Tribeca Productions produced the movie, the party featured Dick Morris and an especially pleased and excited Richard Butler, who was described by an eyewitness as "glistening." Mr. Morris was Mr. Clinton's fabled and unscrupulous advisor on matters of public opinion. Mr. Butler was the supervisor of United Nations efforts to disarm Saddam Hussein's despotism. In February 1998, faced with a threatened bombing attack that never came, Iraqi state TV prophylactically played a pirated copy of *Wag the Dog* in prime time. By Christmastime 1998, Washington police officers were giving the shove to demonstrators outside the White House who protested the December 16–19 bombing of Iraq with chants of "Killing children's what they teach—that's the crime they should impeach" and a "No blood for blow jobs" placard.

Is it possible—is it even thinkable—that these factors are in any way related? "In order that he might rob a neighbour whom he had promised to defend," wrote Macaulay in 1846 of Frederick the Great, "black men fought on the coast of Coromandel, and red men scalped each other by the Great Lakes of North America." Did, then, a dirtied blue dress from the Gap cause widows and orphans to set up grieving howls in the passes of Afghanistan, the outer precincts of Khartoum, and the wastes of Mesopotamia? Is there only a Hollywood link between Clinton's carnality and Clinton's carnage? Was our culture hit by weapons of mass distraction? Let us begin with the best-studied case, which is Khartoum.

On August 20, 1998, the night of Monica Lewinsky's return to the grand jury and just three days after his dismal and self-pitying nonapology had "bombed" on prime-time TV, Clinton personally ordered missile strikes against the El Shifa Pharmaceutical Industries Company on the outskirts of Sudan's capital city. The Clinton administration made three allegations about the El Shifa plant:

- That it did not make, as it claimed, medicines and veterinary products.

- That it did use the chemical EMPTA (O-ethyl methylphosphonothioic acid), which is a "precursor," or building block, in the manufacture of VX nerve gas.

- That it was financed by Osama bin Laden—the sinister and fanatical Saudi entrepreneur wanted in connection with lethal attacks on U.S. embassies in Africa—or by his shadowy business empire.

These three claims evaporated with astonishing speed. It was conceded within days, by Defense Secretary William Cohen, that the factory did make medicines, vials of which were filmed as they lay in the rubble. It was further conceded that there was no "direct" financial connection between the plant and bin Laden's holdings. Later came the humbling admission that a local CIA informer in Sudan had been fired for the fabrication of evidence. Later still came the even more humbling refusal to produce the "soil sample," taken from outside the factory, which the Clinton administration claimed contained traces of EMPTA. In the end, the United States was placed in the agonizing position, at the United Nations, of opposing a call for on-site inspection that had been put forward by the Sudanese.

Bad enough, you might think. But this was only the beginning. The British engineer who was technical manager at the time of El Shifa's construction, Mr. Tom Carnaffin, came forward to say that it contained no space for clandestine procedures or experiments. The German ambassador to Khartoum, Werner Daum, sent a report to Bonn saying that he was familiar with the factory—often used as a showcase for foreign visitors—and that it could not be adapted for lethal purposes. R.J.P. Williams, professor emeritus at Oxford University, who has been called the grandfather of bio-inorganic chemistry, told me that even if the soil sample could be produced it would prove nothing. EMPTA can be used to make nerve gas, just as fertilizer can be used to make explosives, but it is also employed in compounds for dealing with agricultural pests. "'Trace' elements in adjacent soil are of no use," Williams said. "We must be told where the compound was found, and in what quantity it is known to have been produced. Either the Clinton administration has something to hide or for some reason is withholding evidence." It was a rout.

Seeking to reassure people, Clinton made a husky speech on Martha's Vineyard eight days after the attack. He looked the audience in the eye and spoke as follows: "I was here on this island up till 2:30 in the morning, trying to make absolutely sure that at that chemical plant there was no night shift. I believed I had to take the action I did, but I didn't want some person who was a nobody to me—but who may have a family to feed and a life to live and probably had no earthly idea what else was going on there—to die needlessly."

At the time, I thought it odd that such a great statesman and general could persuade himself, and attempt to persuade others, that the more deadly the factory, the smaller the chance of its having a night watchman. Silly me. I had forgotten the scene in Rob Reiner's *The American President*, where a widower First Citizen played by Michael Douglas has a manly affair with a woman lobbyist of his own age played by Annette Bening. While trying to impress us with his combination of determination and compassion, this character says, "Somewhere in Libya right now, a janitor is working the night shift at Libyan intelligence headquarters. And he's going about doing his job because he has no idea that in about an hour he's going to die in a massive explosion."

In the event, only one person was killed in the rocketing of Sudan. But many more have died, and will die, because an impoverished country has lost its chief source of medicines and pesticides. (El Shifa made over 60 percent of the human and veterinary medicine in Sudan.) We know that Clinton picked the target, from a "menu" of options, himself. He seems to have had an additional motive of political opportunism, beyond the obvious one, for selecting this particular underdeveloped country. Many Americans know little about Sudan, but some know a great deal. With its ramshackle fundamentalist regime, the Khartoum government is almost number one on the hate list of Southern Christian activists in the United States, who were at this very time loudly demanding an Act of Congress, prohibiting economic intercourse with countries that discriminated against variant monotheisms, especially of the Christian variety. The Clinton administration, which strongly prefers less sentimental trade policies (and which was then on the verge of "de-linking" human rights from its trade and military relationship with China) was nonetheless willing to compromise on this bill. So by choosing a Sudanese target, Clinton was sending a "message" (to use his argot) at least as much to the biblical sectarians among his own voting base as to the Koranic sectarians of the upper Nile. Triangulation could go no further.

The rout continues. In fact, it becomes a shambles. Let us suppose that everything the administration alleged about El Shifa was—instead of embarrassingly untrue—absolutely verifiable. The Sudanese regime has diplomatic relations with Washington. Why not give it a warning or notice of, say, one day to open the plant to inspection? A factory making deadly gas cannot be folded like a tent and stealthily moved away. Such a demand, made publicly, would give pause to any regime that sheltered Mr. bin Laden or his assets. (Of course, his best-known holdings have been in Saudi Arabia, but a surprise Clintonian cruise-missile attack on that country, with the princes finding out the news only when they fiddle with the remote and get CNN, seems improbable, to say the least.) It is this question which has led me to the Ritz-Carlton Hotel on the edge of the Beltway—the non-Monica Ritz-Carlton located within brunching distance of Langley, Virginia—to meet with Milt Bearden.

Mr. Bearden is one of the Central Intelligence Agency's most decorated ex-officers, having retired in 1994 without any stain from assassination plots, black-bag jobs, or the like. During his long service, he was chief of station in Sudan, where he arranged the famous airlift of Ethiopian Jews to Israel. He also directed the CIA effort in Afghanistan. (His excellent new thriller, *The Black Tulip*, carries a 1991 photograph of him standing at the Russian end of the Friendship Bridge, across which the Red Army had marched in defeat.) Nobody knows clandestine Sudan and clandestine Afghanistan in the way he does. We speak on background, but after some fine-tuning he agrees to be quoted in exactly these words: "Having spent thirty years in the CIA being familiar with soil and environmental sampling across a number of countries, I cannot imagine a single sample, collected by third-country nationals and especially by third-country nationals whose country has a common border, serving as a pretext for an act of war against a sovereign state with which we have both diplomatic relations and functioning back channels."

This bald statement contains a lot of toxic material. The local "agents" who collected that discredited soil sample were almost certainly Egyptians, who have a Nilotic interest in keeping Sudan off balance because, as Bearden pun-

gently says, "their river runs through it." Moreover, when the United States
wanted Mr. bin Laden to leave the territory of Sudan, Washington contacted
Khartoum and requested his deportation, which followed immediately. (He
went to Afghanistan.) When the French government learned that Carlos "the
Jackal" was lurking in Sudan, they requested and got his extradition. Business
can be done with the Sudanese regime. What, then, was the hurry last August
20? No threat, no demand, no diplomatic démarche . . . just a flight of cruise
missiles hitting the wrong target. Take away every exploded hypothesis, says
Sherlock Holmes—this time in "The Adventures of the Beryl Coronet"—and
the one you are left with, however unlikely, will be true. Take away all the
exploded claims about Sudan, and the question "What was the hurry?" prac-
tically answers itself.

Can the implication—of lawless and capricious presidential violence—be taken any further? Oh yes, amazingly enough, it can. On more
than one occasion, I have argued the case across Washington dinner tables
with Philip Bobbitt of the National Security Council. He's a nephew of
LBJ, and he tries to trump me by saying that the U.S. does possess evidence of nerve-gas production at El Shifa and "human and signals intelligence" about a bin Laden connection to the Sudanese. But this evidence
cannot be disclosed without endangering "sources and methods"—and
the lives of agents.

Bearden has forgotten more about "sources and methods" than most
people will ever know, and snorts when I mention this objection. "We
don't like to reveal sources and methods, true enough. But we always do
so if we have to, or if we are challenged. To justify bombing [Colonel
Qaddafi] in 1986, Reagan released the cables we intercepted between
Tripoli and the Libyan Embassy in East Berlin. Same with Bush and Iraq.
Do you imagine that the current administration is sitting on evidence

that would prove it right? It's the dogs that don't bark that you have to listen to." And so my canine theme resumes.

In a slightly noticed article in the *New Yorker* of October 12, 1998 (almost the only essay in that journal in the course of the entire twelve months which was not a strenuous, kneepadded defense of the president), Seymour Hersh revealed that the four service chiefs of the Joint Chiefs of Staff had been deliberately kept in the dark about the Sudan and Afghanistan bombings because if they had been consulted they would have argued against them. He further disclosed that Louis Freeh, head of the FBI, was kept "out of the loop." Mr. Freeh, who has clashed with Clinton and with Attorney General Janet Reno over the issue of a special prosecutor for campaign finance, was not delighted to hear of the raids. For one thing, he and many of his agents were already in the field in East Africa, somewhat exposed as to their own security, and were in the course of securing important arrests. They would have greatly appreciated what they did not in fact get: adequate warning of a strike that would enrage many neighboring societies and governments. It's now possible to extend the list of senior intelligence personnel who disapproved both of the bombings and of their timing. At the CIA, I gather, both Jack Downing, the deputy director for operations, and the chief for the Africa Division told colleagues in private that they were opposed. It is customarily very hard to get intelligence professionals to murmur dissent about an operation that involves American credibility. However, it is also quite rare for a cruise-missile strike to occur on an apparent whim, against an essentially powerless country, at a time when presidential credibility is a foremost thought in people's mind.

The Afghanistan attack, which took place on the same night as the Sudan fiasco, is more easily disposed of. In that instance, the Clinton administration announced that Osama bin Laden and his viciously bearded associates were all meeting in one spot, and that there was only one "window" through which to hit them. This claim is unfalsifiable to the same extent that it is unprovable. Grant that, on the run after the embassy bombings, bin Laden and his gang decided it would be smart to foregather in one place, on territory extremely well known to American intelligence.

All that requires explaining is how a shower of cruise missiles did not manage to hit even one of the suspects. The only casualties occurred among regular Pakistani intelligence officers, who were using the "training camps" to equip guerrillas for Kashmir. As a result, indignant Pakistani authorities released two just-arrested suspects in the American Embassy bombings—one Saudi and one Sudanese. (The Saudi citizen, some American sources say, was a crucial figure in the planning for those outrages in Nairobi and Dar es Salaam.) Not great, in other words. One might add that a stray cruise missile didn't even hit Afghanistan but fell on Pakistani territory, thus handing the Pakistani military a free sample just months after it had defied Clinton's feeble appeals to refrain from joining the "nuclear club." All in all, a fine day's work. Pressed to come up with something to show for this expensive farce, the Clintonoids spoke of damage to bin Laden's "infrastructure." Again, to quote Milt Bearden, who knows Afghanistan by moonlight: "What 'infrastructure'? They knocked over a lean-to? If the administration had anything—anything at all—the high-resolution satellite images would have been released by now." Another nonbarking canine, for a president half in and half out of the doghouse.

Speaking of the doghouse, last fall the president's lawyer Bob Bennett gave a speech to the National Press Club in Washington. On a single day—so he informed an openmouthed audience—he had had four substantial conversations with Clinton about the Paula Jones case and, feeling this excessive, "I had to cut it short and the president said, 'Yeah, I've got to get back to Saddam Hussein,' and I said, 'My God, this is lunacy that I'm taking his time on this stuff.'" Well, I hope Mr. Bennett didn't charge for that day, or for the other time-wasting day when he naively introduced Lewinsky's false affidavit on Clinton's behalf. But, if he hoped to persuade his audience that Clinton should be left alone to conduct a well-meditated Iraq policy, his words achieved the opposite effect. Policy toward Baghdad has been without pulse or direction or principle ever since Mr. Clinton took office. As one who spent some horrible days in Halabja, the Kurdish city that was ethnically cleansed by Saddam's chemical bombs, I have followed Washington's recent maneuvers with great attention. The only moment when this president showed a glimmer of interest in the matter was when his own interests were involved as well.

And thus we come to the embarrassing moment last December when Clinton played field marshal for four days, and destroyed the UN inspection program in order to save it. By November 14, 1998, Saddam Hussein had exhausted everybody's patience by his limitless arrogance over inspections of weapon sites, and by his capricious treatment of the United Nations Special Commission (UNSCOM) inspectorate. In a rare show of Security Council solidarity, Russia, China, and France withdrew criticism of a punitive strike. The Republican leadership in both houses of Congress, which had criticized the Clinton administration for inaction, was ready to rock 'n' roll with Iraq. The case had been made, and the airplanes were already in the air when the president called them back. No commander in chief has ever done this before. Various explanations were offered as to why Clinton, and his close political crony Sandy Berger, had made such a wan decision. It was clearly understood that the swing vote had been the president's, and that Madeleine Albright and William Cohen had argued the other way.

But in mid-November the president was still flushed with the slight gain made by his party in the midterm elections. Impeachment seemed a world away, with Republican "moderates" becoming the favorite of headline writers and op-ed performers alike. This theme persisted in the news and in the polls until after the pre-Hanukkah weekend of December 12–13, when, having been rebuffed by Benjamin Netanyahu at a post-Wye visit in Israel, Clinton had to fly home empty-handed. This must have been galling for him, since he had only imposed himself on the original Wye agreement, just before the November elections, as a high-profile/high-risk electoral ploy. (He had carried with him to Tel Aviv, on Air Force One, Rick Lazio and Jon Fox, two Republican congressmen widely hailed as fence-sitters regarding impeachment. So it can't easily be said that he wasn't thinking about the domestic implications of foreign policy.) But by Tuesday, December 15, after Clinton's last-ditch nonapology had "bombed" like all its predecessors, every headline had every waverer deciding for impeachment after all. On Wednesday afternoon, the president announced that Saddam Hussein was, shockingly enough, not complying with the UN inspectorate. And the cruise missiles took wing again. Within hours the House Republicans had met and, "furious and fractured," according to the *New York Times*, had announced the postponement of the impeachment debate, due to begin Thursday morning.

This was not quite like the preceding dramas. For one thing, it could and probably would have happened—unlike Sudan and Afghanistan—at any time. For another thing, the president was careful to say that he had the support of his whole "national security team," which he wouldn't have been able to say of his cop-out decision in November. Presidents don't normally list the number of their own employees and appointees who agree with them about national-security questions, but then, most presidents don't feel they have to. (Though most presidents have avoided making their Cabinet members back them in public on falsehoods about "private" and "inappropriate" conduct.) Having gone on slightly too long about the endorsements he'd won from his own much-bamboozled team, Clinton was faced with only a few remaining questions. These included:

- Why, since Saddam Hussein has been in constant noncompliance, must bombing start tonight?

- Why has there been no open consultation with either Congress or the United Nations?

- When did you find out about the Richard Butler report on Saddam Hussein's violations?

The last question, apparently a simple one, was the most difficult to answer. It emerged that Clinton had known the contents of the Butler report at least two days before it was supposed to be handed to the UN secretary-general, Kofi Annan. It was Kofi Annan's job, furthermore, to present it to the world body for action. Members of the National Security Council in Washington, however, were leaking the report (which "discovered" Saddam Hussein's violations) to friends of mine in Washington by Tuesday, December 15. This timeline simply means that Clinton knew well in advance that he was going to be handed a free pretext in case of need. Mr. Butler might care to explain why he hurriedly withdrew his inspectors without Security Council permission—leaving some 400 United Nations humanitarian aid workers to face the music—at least a day before the bombs began to drop.

Once again the question: What was the rush? It must have meant a lot to Clinton to begin the strikes when he did, because he forfeited the support of the UN, of Russia, of China, of France, and of much of the congressional leadership—all of which he had enjoyed in varying degrees in November. (The Russians, whose volatile stock of "weapons of mass destruction" is far more of a menace than Iraq's, actually withdrew their ambassador from Washington for the first time in history, and threatened again to freeze talks on strategic-arms limitation.)

To the "rush" question, Clinton at first answered that the weekend of December 19–20 marked the start of the Muslim holy month of Ramadan, and one would not want to be bombing an Islamic people while they were beginning their devotions. However, the postponed impeachment debate continued well into Saturday, December 19, and so did the bombardment, which concluded a few hours after the impeachment vote itself. Muslim susceptibilities were therefore even more outraged, even in morally friendly countries such as Kuwait, by the suspicious coincidence of timing. During the debate, the House Democratic leadership took the position, openly encouraged by the White House, that a president should not be embarrassed at home while American troops were "in harm's way" abroad. Again, it is made clear by Clinton's own conduct and arguments that, for him, foreign policy and domestic policy do not exist in parallel universes, but are one and the same.

And, again, I found myself talking to someone who is normally more hawkish than I am. Scott Ritter, who served with UNSCOM from 1991 until August 1998 and who was the chief of its Concealment Investigations Unit, had been warning for months that Saddam Hussein was evading compliance inspections. This warning entailed a further accusation, which was that UNSCOM in general, and Richard Butler in particular, were too much under the day-to-day control of the Clinton administration. (An

Australian career diplomat who, according to some of his colleagues, was relinquished with relief by his masters Down Under, Butler owes his job to Madeleine Albright in the first place.) Thus, when the United States did not want a confrontation with Iraq, over the summer and into the fall, Butler and the leadership acted like pussycats and caused Ritter to resign over their lack of seriousness. But then, when a confrontation was urgently desired in December, the slightest pretext would suffice. And that, Ritter says, is the bitterest irony of all. The December strikes had no real military value, because the provocation was too obviously staged.

"They sent inspectors to the Baath Party HQ in Baghdad in the week before the raids," Ritter told me. "UNSCOM then leaves in a huff, claiming to have been denied access. There was nothing inside that facility anyway. The stuff was moved before they got there. The United States knew there was nothing in that site. And then a few days later, there are reports that cruise missiles hit the Baath Party HQ! It's completely useless. Butler knew that I'd resign if the U.S. continued to jerk UNSCOM around, and he even came to my leaving party and bought me a drink. But now he's utterly lost his objectivity and impartiality, and UNSCOM inspections have been destroyed in the process, and one day he'll be hung out to dry. Ask your colleagues in Washington when they got his report."

From the *Washington Post* account by Barton Gellman, on Wednesday, December 16, written the day before the bombing began and on the day that Kofi Annan saw the Butler report for the first time:

> Butler's conclusions were welcome in Washington, which helped orchestrate the terms of the Australian diplomat's report. Sources in New York and Washington said Clinton-administration officials played a direct role in shaping Butler's text during multiple conversations with him Monday at secure facilities in the U.S. mission to the United Nations.

"Of course," Ritter told me almost conversationally, "though this is *Wag the Dog*, it isn't quite like Sudan and Afghanistan in August, which were *Wag the Dog* pure and simple."

Well, indeed, nothing is exactly like *Wag the Dog*. In the movie, the whole war is invented and run out of a studio, and nobody actually dies, whereas in Sudan and Afghanistan and Iraq, real corpses were lying about and blood spilled. You might argue, as Clinton's defenders have argued in my hearing, that if there was such a "conspiracy" it didn't work. To this there are three replies. First, no Clinton apologist can dare, after the victim cult sponsored by both the president and the First Lady, to ridicule the idea of "conspiracy," vast or otherwise. Second, the bombings helped to raise Clinton's poll numbers and to keep them high, and who will say that this is not a permanent White House concern? Third, the subject was temporarily changed from Clinton's thing to Clinton's face, and doubtless that came as some species of relief. But now we understand what in November was a mystery. A much less questionable air strike was canceled because, at that time, Clinton needed to keep an "option" in his breast pocket.

On January 6, two weeks after I spoke to Scott Ritter, UN secretary-general Kofi Annan's office angrily announced that, under Richard Butler's leadership, UNSCOM had in effect become a wholly owned subsidiary of the Clinton administration. The specific disclosure concerned the organization's spying activities, which had not been revealed to the UN. But Ritter's essential point about UNSCOM's and Butler's subservient client role was also underscored. This introduces two more canines—the UN inspectors being metamorphosed from watchdogs into lapdogs.

The staged bombing of Iraq in December was in reality the mother of all pinpricks. It was even explained that nerve-gas sites had not been hit, lest the gas be released. (Odd that this didn't apply in the case of the El

Shifa plant, which is located in a suburb of Khartoum.) The Saddam Hussein regime survived with contemptuous ease, while its civilian hostages suffered yet again. During the prematurely triumphant official briefings from Washington, a new bureaucratic euphemism made its appearance. We were incessantly told that Iraq's capacities were being "degraded." This is not much of a target to set oneself, and it also leads to facile claims of success, since every bomb that falls has by definition a "degrading" effect on the system or the society. By acting and speaking as he did, not just in August but also in December, Clinton opened himself, and the United States, to a charge of which a serious country cannot afford even to be suspected. The tin pots and yahoos of Khartoum and Kabul and Baghdad are micro-megalomaniacs who think of their banana republics as potential superpowers. It took this president to "degrade" a superpower into a potential banana republic.

*   *   *

So overwhelming was the evidence in the case of the Sudanese atrocity that by January 1999 it had become a serious embarrassment to the Clinton administration. The true owner of the El Shifa plant, a well-known Sudanese entrepreneur named Saleh Idris, approached Dr. Thomas Tullius, head of the chemistry department at Boston University, and asked him to conduct a forensic examination of the site. Samples taken from all levels, and submitted to three different laboratories in different world capitals, yielded the same result. There were no traces of any kind of toxicity, or indeed of anything but standard pharmaceutical material. Armed with this and other evidence, Mr. Idris demanded compensation for his destroyed property and initiated proceedings for a lawsuit. His case in Washington was taken up by the law firm of Akin, Gump, Strauss, Hauer and Feld—perhaps best known for the prominence with which Vernon Jordan adorns its board of partners.

As a capitalist and holder of private property, Mr. Idris was always likely to receive due consideration if he was prepared to hire the sorts of help that are understood in the Clintonoid world of soft money and discreet law firms. The worker killed at the plant, the workers whose livelihood depended upon it, and those further down the stream whose analgesics and antibiotics never arrived, and whose names are not recorded, will not be present when the recompenses are agreed. They were expendable objects of Clinton's ruthless vanity.

NOTE

On 27 October 1999, *The New York Times* finally published an entire page of reportage, under the byline of Jame Risen, disclosing extensive official misgiving about the Al-Shifa atrocity. Under the subheading "After the Attack, Albright and Top Aid Killed Critical Report," it was revealed that a report from the State Department's Bureau of Intelligence and Research, which cast serious doubt on any connection between the plant and either Bin-Laden or the manufacture of chemical weapons, had been suppressed by Ms. Albright and her Under Secretary of State Thomas Pickering. Several highly placed diplomatic and intelligence chieftains were quoted by name as sharing in the view that Al-Shifa was not a legitimate target. *The New York Times* did not, however, see fit to ask what the urgency had been, or to discompose its readers by mentioning what else had been on the presidential mind that week.

SIX

IS THERE A RAPIST IN THE OVAL OFFICE?

Some years ago, after the disappearance of civil rights workers Chaney,
Goodman, and Schwirner in Mississippi, some friends of mine were
dragging the rivers for their bodies. This one wasn't Schwirner. This one
wasn't Goodman. This one wasn't Chaney. Then, as Dave Dennis tells it,
"It suddenly struck us—what difference did it make that it wasn't them?
What are these bodies doing in the river?"

That was nineteen years ago. The questions has not been answered,
and I dare you to go digging in the bayou.
—James Baldwin, Evidence of Things Not Seen, *1985*

ON 14 DECEMBER 1999, quite uncarried by the networks (though it was
filmed and televised locally) and almost unreported in the so-called "pencil
press" or print media, there occurred the following astonishing moment.
Vice President Albert Gore Jr was holding a "town meeting" in Derry, New
Hampshire when a woman named Katherine Prudhomme stood up to ask:

> When Juanita Broaddrick made the claim, which I found to be quite cred-
> ible, that she was raped by Bill Clinton, did that change your opinion

about him being one of the best presidents in history? And do you believe
Juanita Broaddrick's claim? And what did you tell your son about this?

THE VICE PRESIDENT (with a nervous giggle): Well, I don't know what to make
of her claim, because I don't know how to evaluate that story, I really don't.

MS. PRUDHOMME Did you see the interview?

THE VICE PRESIDENT No, I didn't see the interview. No. Uh-uh.

MS. PRUDHOMME I'm very surprised that you didn't watch the interview.

THE VICE PRESIDENT Well, which show was it on?

MS. PRUDHOMME ABC, I believe.

THE VICE PRESIDENT I didn't see it. There have been so many personal allegations and such a non-stop series of attacks, I guess I'm like a lot of people in that I think enough is enough. I do not know how to evaluate each
one of these individual stories. I just don't know. I would never violate the
privacy of my communication with one of my children, a member of my
family, as for that part of your question. But—

MS. PRUDHOMME So you didn't believe Juanita Broaddrick's claim?

THE VICE PRESIDENT No I didn't say that. I said I don't know how to evaluate
that, and I didn't see the interview. But I must say something else to you
about this. Why don't you just stand back up; I'd like to look you in the eye.
I think that whatever mistakes [Clinton] made in his personal life are in the
minds of most Americans balanced against what he has done in his public
life as president. My philosophy, since you asked about my religious faith, I'm
taught in my religious tradition to hate the sin and love the sinner. I'm
taught that all of us are heir to the mistakes that - are prone to the mistakes
that flesh is heir to. And I think that, in judging his performance as a president, I think that most people are anxious to stop talking about all the personal attacks against him. And trying to sort out all of the allegations, and

want to, instead, move on and focus on the future. Now I'll say this to you, he is my friend, and that friendship is important, and if you've ever had a friend who made a serious mistake and then you repaired the friendship and moved on, then you know what that relationship has been like for me.

Secondly, I felt the same disappointment and anger at him during the period when all this was going on that most people did. You may have felt a different kind of emotion, I don't know. I sense that maybe you did. I certainly felt what most Americans did.

Third, I have been involved in a lot of battles where he and I have fought together on behalf of the American people, and I think we've made a good, positive difference for this country.

Number four, I'm running for president on my own. I want to take my own values of faith and family to the presidency, and I want you to evaluate me on the basis of who I am and what you believe I can do for this country as president. Thank you.

And thank *you*, too, Mr. Vice-President. Innumerable grotesqueries strike the eye, even as it glides over this inert expanse of boilerplate evasion and unction. Mr. Gore is evidently seeking to identify himself painlessly with "most" (four repetitions) of the public. Yet he also feels a vague need to assert courage and principle and thus asks his lone lady questioner (who has properly resumed her seat) to stand up and be looked in the eye. Such gallantry! He then tells her that "since you asked about my religious faith"—which she had not—she is entitled to some pieties, in which he proceeds to misremember *Hamlet* rather than the Sermon on the Mount.

But all of this is paltry detail when set against the one arresting, flabbergasting, inescapable realization. For the first time in American history, a sitting Vice President has been asked whether or not there is a rapist in the Oval Office. A Vice President with "access" to boot, and a likely nominee for the same high position. A Vice President who has described the incumbent as a close friend. And he replies, at inhuman length, that he doesn't really know!

The despicable euphemisms he deploys only serve to emphasize the echoing moral emptiness: if Clinton made the "mistake" with Ms. Broaddrick that the lady questioner alleges, it was an intervention in *her* "personal life," not his. This is where we live now, in the room-temperature ethics of the 2000 election. But more astonishing still is what is *not said*. In the course of a lengthy, drivelling, and alternately obsequious and blustering response, the President's eight-year understudy, close colleague, self-confessed friend, and would-be successor will not say that he disbelieves this foulest of all allegations. He twice mumbles that he cannot "evaluate" the charge of rape. Most of the male readers of this article, I hope and believe, would expect even their nodding acquaintances to do better than that for them. The question of "which show was it on?" is, in the circumstances, rather beside the point. Most politicians in any case either do watch NBC's *Dateline* (Ms. Prudhomme was in error about the network) or have their researchers watch it for them. It's a popular and respected and well-produced show. "Most Americans" who did watch it, in March 1999, concluded that Juanita Broaddrick was unlikely to be lying. Mr. Gore must have read at least that much in the press; his arranging to be adequately uninformed about the story—his positively freakish lack of curiosity—must therefore have taken him some trouble. An open mind need not be an empty mind—though in some cases one is compelled to wonder.

And one can often tell a good deal from an initial reaction, in which the affectation of innocence is present, yet present in such a way as to arouse or confirm suspicion. Take the following excerpt from Roger Morris's book *Partners in Power: The Clintons and Their America*, published in 1996. On page 238 appears the following story:

> A young woman lawyer in Little Rock claimed that she was accosted by
> Clinton when he was attorney general and that when she recoiled he

forced himself on her, biting and bruising her. Deeply affected by the assault, the woman decided to keep it all quiet for the sake of her hard-won career and that of her husband. When the husband later saw Clinton at the 1980 Democratic Convention, he delivered a warning. "If you ever approach her," he told the governor, "I'll kill you." Not even seeing fit to deny the incident, Bill Clinton sheepishly apologized and duly promised never to bother her again.

Roger Morris, who resigned from the National Security Council in protest at the Vietnam war, and who has since authored an acclaimed and garlanded critical biography of Richard Nixon, is not from the ranks of the traditional Clinton haters or right-wing sleuths. (Not that one would exactly relish being called a Clinton-*lover*, either.) He invites us to notice what Clinton did *not* say when accosted. Most male readers of these pages, I again hope and trust, would react differently if approached by an irate man and threatened with deadly force if they so much as approached his wife again. Normal, human reaction? "I don't know what you're talking about" or "Are you sure you know who you're addressing?" Clinton reaction: "OK, OK, I'll stay away from her . . . "

I've talked to Morris at length about the incident, and he agreed to relay messages to and from the couple concerned, to go over his real-time notes with me, to put his own reputation behind the story and to do every-thing, in short, except reveal the identity of the woman. (Keep your eye on that last point, which will recur.) Here's what happened. In the summer of 1993 he had been commissioned by Henry Holt, one of America's most lib-eral publishers, to do a book on Clinton's first hundred days:

> I went down to Little Rock and started cold: most of my friends were
> liberal lawyers from Common Cause and I started with the local
> contacts they gave me. A young attorney from Hot Springs took me

aside one evening and said that, for all the jokes and rumors about
Clinton's sex life, not all the encounters had been consensual. He
gave me the name of one young woman in particular. When I called
her at her office she stonewalled me completely but then her husband telephoned me at the Camelot Hotel and said: "We'll talk; but
it's off the record."

At that time, Arkansas had a freshly-anointed President to boast of; the
well-to-do in Little Rock were not anxious to be making disagreeable
waves. Morris went to a family home in the upscale part of the town and
found two prosperous and well-educated lawyers, the woman from
Arkansas and the husband from a neighboring Southern state.

> She was still frightened while he, I would say, was still furious. The inci-
> dent had occurred about the time when they were getting married, and
> they'd since had children. From the photos on the mantelpiece and
> around the place, I could see that they were well-connected locally, and
> they talked as if social as well as family embarrassment might be involved
> in any publicity. I thought they might be taking themselves much too
> seriously; even over-dramatizing things. And I also thought—come on.
> Clinton may be sleazy but he's not an *ogre* for Christ's sake.

Morris asked the woman the mandatory questions: Did he think you
were coming on to him? Were there mixed signals? Was this just a bad
date, or a misunderstanding? However, the woman later called him and
arranged to meet in a roadhouse barbeque joint on the far outskirts of
town. She still wished, she said, that no one had ever found out. But she'd
had to tell one or two people the following:

> She told me it took place in "a work situation," but after work. She'd
> been working on his campaign, not in his Arkansas government office.
> When I asked her "were you interested or were you attracted?" she said

definitely not, she already had a man and was on the cusp of marriage. At a party in a campaign supporter's home they were left alone after the main crowd had departed and he suddenly got very nasty—threw her down, forced her, bit her hard on the mouth and face . . . She told me she felt more disgraced than violated.

Professional investigators on police rape squads learn to recognize an MO in these matters, and the biting of the lip or the face was also the specialized, distinctive feature in the case of Juanita Broaddrick. It is important to stress, here, that neither Ms. Broaddrick nor the woman in the Morris biography can possibly have known of each other's existence, or in any way concerted their separate stories, at the time they told them. Here, in its extensively corroborated detail, is the testimony of Juanita Broaddrick:

In the spring of 1978 Juanita Hickey (as she was then known during her first marriage) was a registered nurse running a nursing home in the town of Van Buren, Arkansas. Clinton was the state's attorney general, and much engaged in his first run for the governorship. Impressed by his candidacy, Juanita (as I'll now call her) volunteered to hand out bumper stickers and signs, and first met the aspiring governor when he made a campaign stop at her nursing home. "While he was there visiting, he said, 'If you're ever in the Little Rock area, please drop by our campaign office . . . be sure and call me when you come in.'" (A photograph of this first meeting exists: it shows a personable Juanita and a young Clinton looking like someone auditioning for a Bee-Gees look-a-like contest.) On 25 April 1978 Juanita was in Little Rock for a nursing home convention held at the Camelot Hotel, and she did call him. He said that after all he wouldn't be at the campaign office so "Why don't I just meet you for coffee in the Camelot coffee shop?" She agreed to this, and also to a later call from him which proposed, since he said there were reporters in the coffee shop, that they meet instead in her hotel room.

> "I had coffee sitting on a little table over there by the window. And
> it was a real pretty window view that looked down at the river. And he
> came around me and sort of put his arm over my shoulder to point to
> this little building. And he said that he was real interested, if he became
> governor, to restore that little building, and then all of a sudden, he
> turned me around and started kissing me . . . I first pushed him away
> . . . Then he tries to kiss me again. And the second time he tries to kiss
> me, he starts biting on my lip . . . He starts to bite on my top lip, and I
> try to pull away from him. And then he forces me down on the bed.
> And I just was very frightened . . . It was a real panicky, panicky situa-
> tion. And I was even to the point where I was getting very noisy, you
> know, yelling to—you know—to please stop. But that's when he would
> press down on my right shoulder and he would bite on my lip."

Her skirt was torn at the waist, her pantyhose ripped at the crotch, and the
attorney-general of Arkansas forced an entry.

> When everything was over with and he got up and straightened himself,
> and I was crying at the moment, and he walks to the door and calmly
> puts on his sunglasses. And before he goes out the door he says "You'd
> better get some ice on that." And he turned and went out the door.

The advice about ice turned out to be sound, according to Juanita's friend
Norma Kelsey who had come along for the trip, who knew that a meeting
with Clinton was planned, and who found Juanita in tears with a badly
swollen lip and ripped pantyhose. She is one of five real-time witnesses to
whom Juanita told the story while her injuries were still visible, the others (all of whom have testified to this effect) being Susan Lewis, Louise
Mah, Jean Darby (the sister of Norma Kelsey) and her husband-to-be,
David Broaddrick. At the time, it is important to mention, she was carrying on a love affair with Mr. Broaddrick and hoped to escape her first

marriage and become his wife. This supplied (a.) a disincentive for casual dalliance with the candidate, of the sort his less tasteful supporters have been known to suggest, and (b.) an additional incentive to keep quiet and avoid scandal. All of her friends also urged her to maintain silence because nobody, in the Arkansas of the time, would believe her.

NBC News possesses great fact-checking resources, and did not air its interview with the highly-convincing Juanita until after an exhaustive process of inquiry. It established her whereabouts on the day in question, even confirming that the view from the hotel bedroom would have been as she described it. There should have been no difficulty in establishing the whereabouts of a state attorney general on any given day: records and appointment books are kept and of course the presumption of innocence suggests that a politician will be eager to help establish an alibi. But according to Lisa Myers, the much-respected correspondent on the story:

> Was Bill Clinton even in Little Rock on April 25 1978? *Despite our repeated requests, the White House would not answer that question and declined to release any information about his schedule.* So we checked 45 Arkansas newspapers and talked to a dozen former Clinton staffers. We found no evidence that Clinton had any public appearances on the morning in question. Articles in Arkansas newspapers suggest he was in Little Rock that day. (Italics added).

There's one grace-note, to set beside the biting as a kind of Clintonian signature. In 1991, Juanita was at another nursing-home meeting in Little Rock, and was suddenly called out into the hallway to meet the Governor. At least one witness remembers seeing them together, and wondering what they could be talking about. According to Juanita:

> He immediately began this profuse apology, saying "Juanita, I'm so sorry for what I did." He would say things like "I'm not the man that I

> used to be. Can you ever forgive me? What can I do to make things up
> to you?" And I'm standing there in absolute shock and I told him to go
> to hell and I walked off.

She wondered why he had made this clumsy bid for contrition, until, a
short while afterwards, she heard him announce publicly that he was
beginning a campaign for the Democratic nomination for the Presidency.
For this, of course, and on many future occasions, a "new Clinton" would
be required.

By the time that NBC aired its Broaddrick interview—which it with-
held until the impeachment trial was over—the President's defenders
had become hardened to dealing with accusations from outraged females.
They were usually able to imply either that the woman in question was an
ally of the political Right, or on a gold-digging expedition, or a slut of low
character who had probably asked for it, or eager to cash in on a memoir.
None of these tactics would work with Juanita, because she had been a
political supporter of Clinton's, had not asked for or received any money
for her story, did not wish to market a book and had, since her divorce
and remarriage, lived a highly respectable life owning and operating a
horse-farm with her husband. Indeed, she had not in the ordinary sense
"gone public" at all. Rather, she had been "outed" by one of the very few
people she had told who was a Republican. Having at one point gone to
the length of denying the story under oath in order to protect her privacy
and that of her new family, she saw that this was futile and determined
that if the story were to be told it should be told fully and by her. (The lie
under oath resulted from a subpoena from Paula Jones's lawyers, in a
case in which she did not wish to involve herself.)

No forensic or medical or contemporary evidence exists and there were
no direct witnesses, even though the number of immediate aftermath

witnesses is impressive and their evidence consistent. This does not mean that the matter dissolves into the traditional moral neutrality of "he said, she said." For one thing, "she" did not wish to say anything. For another— and here again we are in the eerie territory of the Clintonian psyche— "he" has not denied it. I repeat for emphasis; the President of the United States, plausibly accused of rape by a reputable woman whose story has been minutely scrutinized by a skeptical television network, offers no denial. His private lawyer David Kendall, a man who did not even know Clinton at the time (and a man who had publicly denied that fellatio is a sexual act) issued the following statement on 19 February 1999:

> Any allegation that the President assaulted Mrs Broaddrick more than twenty years ago is absolutely false. Beyond that, we're not going to go.

And beyond that, they haven't gone. Of course the statement is open to Clintonian parsing. *Any* allegation? Oh, you mean *this* allegation? In 1978 the President was Jimmy Carter, who certainly didn't "assault" any woman that year. And in 1978, Juanita was Mrs. Hickey. So—did Bill Clinton rape Mrs. Hickey that year? The question, under White House rules of evidence, has not even been posed yet. (The President has since paid a fine of $90,000 for lying under oath in a Federal Court, and made a payment of $850,000 to settle an allegation of sexual harassment, and has been cited by a DC judge for a criminal violation of the Privacy Act in the matter of Kathleen Willey, so the "he said" element would be weaker than usual in any event.)

The next month, on 19 March, Sam Donaldson of ABC News raised the matter at a press conference and was referred by Clinton to the above lawyer's statement. The President would not even deny the allegation in the first person, or in his own voice. "Can you not simply deny it, sir?" asked Donaldson plaintively. And answer came there none.

It is just possible that the Broaddrick scandal, despite having been dropped by a generally compliant press, is not yet over. On 16 December 1999, Lanny Davis, one of the President's more sinuous apologists, was asked on an MSNBC chat show to address the issue and replied that Ms. Broaddrick had been adjudged unreliable by the FBI. "How do you know, Lanny?" he was asked, and had no immediately very convincing answer, since her FBI file, if any, would be none of his business. On 20 December, Juanita Broaddrick filed a suit in Federal District Court seeking any files on her kept by the White House or the Justice Department. The White House responds that "there will be no comment" from them on this legal initiative by a private citizen who might be said to have suffered enough.

If Juanita Broaddrick is not telling the truth, then she is either an especially cruel and malicious liar, who should at a minimum be sued for defamation, or a delusional woman who should be seeking professional help. Nobody who has met or spoken with her believes that these necessary corollaries obtain even in the slightest way. And on this occasion, we can't just lazily say that it's her (not unsupported) word against that of a proven liar, because the proven liar hasn't even cared, or do I mean dared, to open his mouth.

For mentioning this squalid subject on TV and radio, I have once or twice been accused of being "obsessed" by Clinton's rape victims. That's neat of course, and typical of his political bodyguards; in their minds nothing is his fault and it's only his accusers who have any explaining to do. But in the third case I know about, which is so far unpublished anywhere, the story came to me without my asking, let alone soliciting. I was in San Francisco, and got a call and later a visit from a very well-known Bay Area journalist and editor. He's a veteran radical and was once quite a Clinton fan; we'd argued about the man before. He wanted, he said, to disburden himself of the following information.

He (I can't give his name without identifying her) had once employed a young female assistant. In the early 1970s, Bill Clinton had come out to the Bay Area to see his fiancé Hillary, who was then working, for some other friends of mine as it happens, as a legal intern in Oakland. An introduction occurred between young Bill and my friend's aforementioned assistant. He asked her out for lunch; she accepted. He proposed a walk in Golden Gate Park; she accepted that too. He made a lunge at her; she declined the advance and was rammed, very hard indeed, against a tree-trunk before being rolled in the bushes and badly set-upon. She's a tall and strong woman, and got away without submitting. She told my friend the same day, and he'd kept the secret for almost thirty years. In those days, girls on the Left were proud of being the equals of men, and took the rough, so to speak, with the smooth. It wasn't done to whine or complain, let alone to go to the forces of law and order, or of repression as they were then known.

Years later, the woman was sitting at her desk when she got a telephone call from Brooke Shearer, who is also Mrs. Strobe Talbott and a veteran of the Clinton kitchen-cabinet. "Bill is thinking of running for office," said Ms. Shearer. "He wanted to know if that was all right with you." My subject was annoyed, but she had retained her old liberal allegiances. She also—see how this keeps coming up?—was thinking of getting engaged and becoming a mother. She replied that she wouldn't stand in the way of a Clinton candidacy. But I have since talked to two further very respectable San Francisco citizens, who have heard her relate the identical story at their own dinner table, and who have neither met nor heard of my original informant (nor he of them). I know the woman's name; I know that she has married well; I know her maiden name at the time of the assault; I know the high-powered Bay Area foundation where she works on good causes; I have communicated with her by Federal Express and by voicemail. I have excellent witnesses who have heard her say that if the story ever breaks she'll deny it under oath. I don't blame her—though in our present unshockable moral atmosphere it's very unlikely that reporters, let alone prosecutors, would even turn over in bed before consigning the whole thing to the memory hole. It is time, as we keep hearing, to put the country behind us and move this forward. (At least, I *think* I've got that right.)

There are several other documented or partly-sourced allegations of rape against this President, and many more allegations of biting and of brutish sexual conduct. Some of these seem to me to be scurrilous, and some that are not scurrilous could be the result of copycat publicity. But the three stories above are untainted in this way, and they seem to leave Juanita Broaddrick, for the moment, with a very strong *prima facie* case.

Circumstantial evidence, as Justice Holmes once phrased it, is often very powerful (and can be used for an indictment or a conviction) precisely because *it is the hardest to arrange.* What are the chances that three socially and personally respectable women, all three of them political supporters of Mr. Clinton and none of them known to each other, would confect or invent almost identical experiences which they did not desire to make public? And how possible would it be for a network of anti-Clinton rumor-mongers to create, let alone ventilate, such a coincidence? The odds that any of these ladies is lying seem to me to approach zero; their reasons for reticence are all perfectly intelligible.

Reticence and feminine discretion, sometimes used to discredit women who don't come forward in time, or at all, are in fact the ally of the perp, as the feminist movement used to instruct us. Indeed, voting against the confirmation of Clarence Thomas to the Supreme Court in 1991, Senator Albert Gore said with almost pompous gravity: "Every woman who has ever struggled to be heard over a society that too often ignores even their most painful calls for justice—we simply cannot take for granted that the victim, or the woman, is always wrong." *Even* their *most* painful? Judge Thomas's accuser said that he had talked dirty to her; no more, even while (if you remember) she'd continued to work for and support him. That didn't stop then-Governor Clinton from denouncing President Bush as "anti-woman" for his disbelief in Professor Hill's charges.

If it was "time to speak out" then, as Hillary Clinton said in presenting Anita Hill with an award, then it's time to speak out now. The same Al Gore has been unable to repress a feeling that there might be something in what Juanita Broaddrick told us. And she tells me that she still cries every time she sees Clinton's gloating face on the TV. The official feminist leadership has forgotten what it used to affirm—which is how seldom decent women lie about rape and how often they bite their lips and keep silent for fear of being defamed or disbelieved. Biting their own lips is still better than having them furiously and lovelessly bitten; is our society so dulled that we simply pass the ice-bag and turn to other things?

Taken together with his silence on the legal lynching of Rickey Ray Rector, and the numb acceptance of the criminal Strangelove bombings of Sudan and Iraq, the mute reception of Juanita Broaddrick's charges illuminates the expiring, decadent phase of American liberalism.

SEVEN

THE SHADOW OF THE CON MAN
Rodham's Last Hurrah

'When you come right down to it, there are only two points that really count.'
    'Such as?'
    Skeffington held up to two fingers. 'One,' he said, ticking the first, "all Ireland must be free." 'Two,' he said, ticking the second, "Trieste belongs to Italy." They count. At the moment the first counts more than the second, but that's only because the Italians were a little slow in getting to the boat.'
    —Edwin O'Connor, *The Last Hurrah*

CYRIL: *Lying! I should have thought that our politicians kept up that habit.*
VIVIAN: *I assure you that they do not. They never rise beyond the level of misrepresentation, and actually condescend to prove, to discuss, to argue. How different from the true liar, with his frank, fearless statements, his superb irresponsibility, his healthy, natural disdain of proof of*

any kind! After all, what is a fine lie? Simply that which is its own evi-
dence. If a man is sufficiently unimaginative to produce evidence in sup-
port of a lie, he might just as well speak the truth at once. No, the
politicians won't do. Something may, perhaps, be urged on behalf of the
Bar. The mantle of the Sophist has fallen on its members. Their feigned
ardors and unreal rhetoric are delightful.
　　—Oscar Wilde, *The Decay of Lying*

TWO FULL TERMS of Clintonism and of "triangulation," and of loveless but dogged bipartisanship, reduced the American scene to the point where politicians had become to politics what lawyers had become to the law: professionalized parasites battening on an exhausted system that had lost any relationship to its original purpose (democracy or popular sovereignty in the first instance; justice or equity in the second). The permanent political class and its ancillaries held all the cards by the 2000 campaign, controlled all the money, decided on all the predigested questions in all the manipulated polls. They did their job almost too well, leaving insufficient room for illusion and inadequate grounds for maintaining any steady or principled party allegiance. As a result, the only realists were the cynics. And this in turn permitted some alarming honesties to be committed in public.

Towards the opening of the campaign season, and on the cusp of an anti-climactic and apathetic millennium, Norman Podhoretz wrote a very striking cover essay for *National Review*. In this article, the former editor of *Commentary* sought to persuade the fans of William F. Buckley that Bill Clinton was not really all that bad. Mr. Podhoretz of course had made his name as a campaigner for the "neo-conservative" opinion that the origins of all moral rot lie in "The Sixties." With his wife Midge Decter and his gifted polemicist son John, and by means of a nexus of other family and political filiations on the Right, he had inveighed against anti-war and anti-imperialist groups, against homosexuals and feminists, against cultural pluralism and anything smacking of the dreaded "correctness." He was one of the many prominent conservative Jews willing to countenance a pact with the Christian Coalition.

Staying at least partly in character, Podhoretz stipulated rather matter-of-factly that Clinton was of course a liar, a crook, a traitor to friends and family alike, a drug-user, a perjurer, a hypocrite, and all the rest of it. However, he argued, this could be set against his one great and unarguable achievement, which was the destruction of "McGovernism" in the Democratic Party. Clinton might, said Podhoretz, have wavered occasionally on matters like the sell-out to China. But he had forever defeated the liberal, union-minded, bleeding heart and environmentalist faction, of the sort that had once stuck up for Vietnamese or Nicaraguans or (worst of all) Palestinians:

> Bill Clinton is a scoundrel and a perjurer and a disgrace to the office he has held. Yet it is this scoundrel, this perjurer, this disgrace to the Presidency of the United States who has pushed and pulled his party into moving in a healthier direction than it had been heading in since its unconditional surrender to the left nearly thirty years ago. As if this were not extraordinary enough in itself, the explanation for it can be found in the very defects of Clinton's character I have just listed.
>
> In my experience, very few politicians have solid principles that they are unwilling to sell out for the sake of winning elections. They are, most them, 'the hollow men, the stuffed men' of whom T. S. Eliot wrote, and in Clinton we have perhaps as extreme an embodiment of this professional deformation as can be unearthed. If he had been a man of any principles at all, a man with something inside him besides the lust for power (and the other lusts that power contributes to satisfying) he

would have been incapable of betraying the people and the ideas he was supposed to represent. If he had not been so great a liar, he would have been unable to get away not only with his own private sins but with the political insults he was administering to some of his core constituencies. And if he had not been such a disgrace to the presidency, he would not have been impeached, and would not thereby have forced even the intransigent McGovernites of his party who had every reason to hate him, into mobilizing on his behalf for fear of the right-wing conspiracy they fantasized would succeed him.

The admission that Clinton is a political conservative, who has moved the Democratic Party to the right while relying on rather prostituted "correctness" constituencies, is one that few authentic conservatives allow themselves. The concession does, however, show an understanding of "triangulation" and it does possess some explanatory power. By the spring of 2000, it was clear that the liberal pulse of the party was to all intents and purposes undetectable. Even former Senator Bill Bradley, returning to the hustings after marinating for a while in the casks of Wall Street, looked discountenanced by the utter failure of the patient to respond. And he was only seeking to awaken the liberal reformist instinct in its mildest and most manageable form. He didn't even brush the G-spot.

Indeed, in what had begun as a rather stilted and fixed campaign, the only outlet for insurgent feeling was that offered in a Republican primary by the eccentric Senator from Arizona. John McCain achieved at least an initial burst of speed by his proclaimed dislike of the system, by his professed distaste for campaign-finance racketeering and by his (apparently) unscripted and unspun style. It was puerile anti-politics but it worked for a space, and drew for its effect on many voters who had registered as Democrats or independents. Nowhere within the echoing emptiness of the Democratic fold was there any hint of a live dialogue. And McCain, of course, had voted to impeach and to convict Clinton, and had gravely upset Governor Bush of Texas, in the course of the South Carolina primary, by comparing him to incumbent President. ("You don't," said Bush in a tone of outrage, "you just don't say that of a man.")

Meanwhile Vice President Gore rather noticeably did not ask his boss to campaign for him, and was often ridiculed for the campaign-finance fiascos and lies in which Clinton had involved him, and discovered that he had all along been very downcast by the President's selfish and thoughtless conduct—never exactly specified, but wincingly hinted at. Looking somewhat like (and very much resembling) a dog being washed, Mr. Gore also feigned excitement at the local campaign he and his backers liked the least: the decision by Hillary Rodham Clinton—the other half of a "buy one, get one free" sleazy lawyer couple—to try and succeed to the vacant Senatorship from the great state of New York.

Everything about this campaign, and everything about this candidate, was rotten from the very start. Mrs. Clinton has the most unappetizing combination of qualities to be met in many days' march: she is a tyrant and a bully when she can dare to be, and an ingratiating populist when that will serve. She will sometimes appear in the guise of a "strong woman" and sometimes in the softer garb of a winsome and vulnerable female. She is entirely un-self-critical and quite devoid of reflective capacity, and has never found that any of her numerous misfortunes or embarrassments are her own fault, because the fault invariably lies with others. And, speaking of where things lie, she can in a close contest keep up with her husband for mendacity. Like him, she is not just a liar but a lie; a phoney construct of shreds and patches and hysterical, self-pitying, demagogic improvisations.

In the early days of her campaign, and just before (this following a clumsy fan-dance of inordinate length) its formal announcement, even her staunchest backers at the *New Yorker* were manifesting alarm. Her kind of slithery rhetoric, wrote the devoted Elizabeth Kolbert, would not quite do. An instance from an address to the Democrats of Westchester County:

> What's important to me are the issues. I mean, who, at the end of the day, is going to improve education for the children of New York? Who's going to improve health care for the people of New York? Who's going to bring people together? And that's what I'm going to be talking about.

Mrs. Clinton's standards were not set high ("improve" instead of the once-bold "reform"? And a Senator "bringing people together," instead of vigorously representing them?) But Ms. Kolbert's standards were not high, either. (Given the chance to ask her candidate a question, she managed to inquire courageously about the difficulty of running as someone from out-of-state, and this as late as January 2000.) But even she had to cringe at the following, delivered to a solidly sympathetic yet bored audience at Riverside Church on the Upper West Side:

> I think it's appropriate to take a few minutes to reflect on some of the issues that people of faith have in common, and from my perspective, as I have traveled extensively through New York and been in the company of New Yorkers from so many different walks of life, I agree that the challenges before us, as individuals, as members and leaders of the community of faith, as those who already hold positions of public responsibility and those who seek them, that we do all share and should be committed to an understanding of how we make progress, but we define that progress, deeply and profoundly.

This, in a prepared text, where even the bored annotators didn't bother to notice that progress was defined as both deep and profound. (Not unlike Vice President Gore's robotic assurance that his use of marijuana had been "infrequent and rare.") Liars can often be detected in that latter way, brashly asserting more than has been asked of them: Mrs. Clinton's chloroform rhetoric is an indication of another kind of falsity; one that is so congested with past lies and evasions—and exposures—that it can only hope to stay alive on the podium by quacking out the clock, ducking or stunning the "question period" and saying nothing testable or original or courageous. This is not, as the *New Yorker* would have us believe, a problem of dynamism or a lapse in the all-important "presentation." And the once-proud New York Democratic Party had actually asked for all this. In the clumsy, sycophantic words of Representative Charles Rangel, whose original idea it was: the party "pulled together an offer that the First Lady can't refuse": the offer of a coronated nomination without any primary contest. "You can always promise no primary to an 800-pound gorilla," said the Congressman stupidly to the New York Times, as if the short-circuiting of voter choice was an achievement to beam about. (We don't have the First Lady's reaction to the primate or the weight comparison: a mirthless grin probably covered it.)

The "Hillary" campaign was inaugurated by a positive Niagara of dishonesty and deceit, much of it related to that most base and obvious pander of the New York politico—the conscription of ethnic politics. New York Jews are hardened by now to the most shameless promises; New York Puerto Ricans perhaps somewhat less so: both constituencies were to receive double-barreled insults to their intelligence almost before the bandwagon had begun to roll. Mr. Clinton had decided to pardon and release some Puerto Ricans nationalists, imprisoned for placing indiscriminate bombs in lower Manhattan; the cause was popular among Puerto Ricans but less favored by other communities. Mrs. Clinton, who almost certainly solicited the favor from a President who almost never employs his power of pardon—and who slew the helpless Rickey Ray Rector—then denounced the clemency when it proved to play badly, and then claimed that she had never discussed any stage of the process with her husband. (On other occasions, she slyly lets on that they have no secrets from each other: the classic alternation of ditsy "little me" housewife and "strong woman.") But "we talk," she had told Tina Brown's *Talk* magazine already. "We talk in the solarium, in the bedroom, in the kitchen—it's just constant conversation." Hard to keep Puerto Rico out of it.

Then, if I may quote myself writing in *The Nation* of May Day 2000, there was the open scandal of the Pakistanian connection:

> Remember when every liberal knew how to sneer at George W. Bush, not only for forgetting the name of Pakistan's new dictator but for saying that he seemed like a good guy? Well, General Musharraf's regime has now hired, at a retainer of $22,500 per month, the DC law firm of Patton Boggs, for which Lanny Davis, one of the First Family's chief apologists, toils. Perhaps for reasons having to do with the separation of powers, Patton Boggs also collects $10,000 monthly from Pak-Pac, the Pakistani lobby in America, for Davis's services in its behalf. Suddenly, no more Dem jokes about ignorance of Pakistan.
>
> Last December, after Clinton announced that Pakistan would not be on his itinerary when he visited the subcontinent, his former White House "special counsel" arranged a fundraiser in Washington at which lawyers from Patton Boggs made contributions to the First Lady's Senate campaign that now total $25,500. So, not very indirectly, Pakistani military money was washed into her coffers from the very start. Then, in February, another Pak-Pac event, in New York, was

brought forward so as to occur before the arrangements for the President's passage to India had been finalized. Having been told that the First Lady did not grace any event for less than $50,000 upfront, the Pakistanis came up with the dough and were handsomely rewarded for their trouble by the presence of Lanny Davis and by a statement from Mrs. Clinton that she hoped her spouse would stop off in Pakistan after all. And a few days later, he announced that, after much cogitation, he would favor General Musharraf with a drop-by.

How does this look to you? One way of deciding it is to try the cover stories on for size. "I wish I could say I had the influence and had applied the right pressure for the President to visit Pakistan, but I didn't, so I can't." That's Lanny Davis. Is this what he tells the Pakistanis in return for his large stipend? "If anybody thinks they can influence the President by making a contribution to me, they are dead wrong." That's Hillary Clinton. Is that what she said at the Pak-Pac fundraiser?

One thing that strikes the eye immediately is how *cheap* this is. And inexpensive, too. The Pakistani nuclear junta must be rubbing its eyes: For such a relatively small outlay of effort it can get the First Family to perform public political somersaults.

The problem with Pakistan is that it is a banana republic with nuclear weapons, run by ambitious and greedy politicians who are scared of their own military-industrial complex. Aren't you glad you don't live there?

As for the Holy Land (the third "I" in the Last Hurrah trilogy of Ireland, Italy, and Israel), Mrs. Clinton came to New York with the uneasy memory of an unscripted remark about the the desirability of a Palestinian state. Eager to live down this momentary embrace of a matter of principle—where else, one wonders, are the Palestinian people to live? Under occupation? In camps? In exile? Even Shimon Peres is for a state by now—she rushed to contradict her husband again, and demand that the United States embassy in Israel be moved forthwith to Jerusalem, before the status of that city has been determined by continuing negotiations. This well-worn pander proposal, set out in a letter to an Orthodox congregation, was somewhat eclipsed by a highly incautious visit to Israel and the occupied territories, in which she sat mutely through a poorly-phrased and paranoid attack on Zionism by Chairman Arafat's first lady. There was therefore nothing for it but the announcement, in August 1999, that Hillary Rodham Clinton had made the joyous discovery of a Jewish step-grandfather on (I hope) her mother's side. For abject currying, this easily outdid the witless and obvious donning of the New York Yankee's cap. Gail Sheehy, not her most critical biographer, tells us that the First Lady has had numerous tucks and lifts and has deployed the magic of liposuction on her thighs and rear end. This is clearly not designed to please her husband; we shall see if it pleases New Yorkers. It may work. More than artifice is involved in the claim made at her 1999 Thanksgiving press conference that: "I don't pay attention to polls." Not long afterwards, a poll was taken about whether Mrs. Clinton should make an appearance on the Late Night show with David Letterman, an invitation to which had been languishing on her mantelpiece for many months. The poll showed that New Yorkers wished she would appear: she duly turned up accompanied by none other than her pollster. Mr. Letterman—as preoccupied as Ms. Kolbert with the "carpet-bagging" non-issue—asked her to name the New York state bird, the state flower and so forth. She answered all the questions correctly; it took a few days before Mr. Letterman admitted that he'd shown her the quiz in advance. Small dishonesties are the reflection of big ones; every trip Mrs. Clinton takes, with sirens blaring and New York traffic brought to a stop, is underwritten by the taxpayer.

That at least cannot be said for the mansion the Clintons bought for themselves in the upscale suburb of Chappaqua. "Bought for themselves" is, in any case, a euphemism: the First Couple is somewhat cleaned out by legal expenses—despite having made use of the Justice Department as private firm—and the $850,000 paid to Paula Jones had to be extracted from the First Lady's blind trust and cattle-futures fund. (One wonders what the "constant conversation" in the family home was like on *that* special morning.) Thus the job of financing the mortgage and closing the deal fell on one single opulent fund-raiser, the egregious Terry McAuliffe. Here again, the entire business was infected with duplicity from the very start. Mr. McAuliffe, who posted the $1.35 million necessary to secure the house in the first place, was at the time facing a grand jury in the matter of some extremely dubious business involving the Teamsters Union. His role in franchising the public rooms of the White House for fund-raisers during the 1996 election (see page 55) almost certainly resulted in the aborting of his nominations as Secretary of Commerce in Clinton's second term. Never before had a sitting President made himself so beholden to an active money-man and influence-peddler. Yet when questions were finally asked, both Clintons stuck mechanically to the line that the Office of Government Ethics had reviewed the deal and found it unobjectionable. Not everybody knows that the Office of Government Ethics is forbidden to answer questions from the press until its report is completed: the brazen lie got the Clintons through the news-cycle of house-purchase and, by the time the Office of Government Ethics had announced that it had said no such thing, the story was well down-page. By that time, also, Mr. McAuliffe's good offices had given way to a bank-loan offered on much more favorable terms than any average citizen can hope to command. And still the drizzle of tiny lies continued: on 16 November 1999, the First Lady's media flack, Howard Wolfson, announced on Larry King Live that the President himself would be moving to the Chappaqua home in the New Year. For a sitting President to quit the Executive Mansion is likewise news: Ms. Hillary when asked about this said blandly "I haven't really talked to him about that." She claimed also that she had not told the President about the announcement of her candidacy—even as that announcement contained the boast that he would be campaigning for her. Only those who are totally habituated to falsehood will so easily and naturally lie when the truth would have done just as well.

It's possible to speculate about whether the First Lady has become such a mistress of mendacity by a sort of osmosis from her husband, and the many levels of "denial" he has imposed upon her, or whether she had the same original talent that he did. (Some objective biographers describe her early shock and alarm at Arkansas Tammany practices, at the discovery of what was considered legal.) Whatever may be the case here, there's no doubt that her single-mindedness, combined with a natural authoritarian self-discipline, have become political phenomena in themselves. Mrs. Clinton may now find it opportune to present herself as a survivor or even a victim, but the the plain facts remain that:

- The hiring of the squalid and unscrupulous Dick Morris, as advisor both at state and national level, was her idea. Mr. Morris has boasted of being a procurer for her husband as part of his package of political skills.

- The hiring of private detectives for the investigation and defamation of inconvenient women was also her idea.

- The dubious use of a powerful law firm as an engine of political patronage was principally her scheme.

- The firing of non-client White House staff, the amassing of files on political opponents, and the magical vanishing and reappearance of subpoenaed documents, all took place in her wing of the White House, and on her apparent instructions.

- A check for $50,000, written by a donor with intimate ties to Chinese military-industrial complex, was hand-delivered to her chief of staff in the White House.

- On a notable occasion, she urged investigative journalists to pursue the rumor that President George Bush had kept a mistress on his payroll.

- She allowed the exploitation of her daughter in the crudest and most painful photo-ops in living memory.

- She regarded the allegation of a sexual arrangement with Monica Lewinsky as proof positive of "a vast right-wing conspiracy."

- She further accused those who pursued that allegation of harboring a prejudice against people from Arkansas, while hailing herself from Illinois, and readying a campaign to represent New York.

- On a visit to New Zealand, she claimed to have been named for Sir Edmund Hillary's ascent of Everest; a triumph that occurred some years after her birth and christening. (I insert this true story partly for comic relief, as showing an especially fantastic sense of self-reinvention as well as a desperate, mysterious willingness to pander for the Kiwi vote.)

A whole chapter could be written under any of these separate headings. Mrs. Clinton, of course, is to be pitied in a way that her husband cannot be. Desperately keen to run him for the nomination in 1988 after the implosion of Gary Hart, she had to debase herself by listening to Betsey Wright's recitation of the roster of outraged women who made that impossible. But this revelation never inhibited her from blaming the female victims; from announcing for example that she would "crucify" Gennifer Flowers, or from helping her spouse to lie his way through that difficulty, and through all the subsequent ones, up to and including believable accusations of rape and molestation.

Her role model, according to herself, is that of Eleanor Roosevelt. She has even claimed, during her remarkably frank admissions of traffic with enablers and facilitators and other modern voodoo-artists, to have "channeled" the former First Lady. Mrs. Roosevelt, who also suffered "pain in her marriage," was constantly urging her husband to be more brave about civil rights, about the threat of fascism, about the plight of the dispossessed. She often shamed him into using some of his credit, with Congress and public opinion, for unpopular causes. There is not one shard of evidence that Mrs. Clinton has ever done any such thing. To the contrary: Dick Morris was her preferred consigliere, and according to him, in 1995 she said:

> Our liberal friends are just going to understand that we have to go for welfare reform—for eliminating the welfare entitlement. They are just going to have to get used to it. I'm not going to listen to them or be sympathetic to them.

At every stage of the fund-raising bonanzas and the stone-walling of special investigators, Mrs. Clinton was at the forefront of the action and found to be urging a more ruthless style. Her reward was to hear Dick Morris say, when he had been fired, that "Bill loves Bill, and Hillary loves Bill, and so that gives them something in common." A sadder dysfunctional bonding would be hard to find: the most bitter and reproachful element being the open and cynical use, in the lying campaign against Jones, Lewinsky, and the other "Jane Does," of Mrs. Clinton's only worthwhile achievement in the shape of her daughter Chelsea. A speck of pity, here, perhaps.

It comes down, though, to the exploitation of mammalian sentiments by reptilian people. When caught making a gigantic profit on cattle-future trades in which she was "carried" by clients of her husband, Mrs. Clinton abandoned the pose of the strong businesswoman perusing the stock pages of the *Wall Street Journal,* and simperingly claimed that her hormones were all out of whack because she was pregnant with Chelsea. How could she be expected to remember details? When the 1996 election looked to be a bit more close-fought than it turned out to be, she artfully told my friend Walter Isaacson, editor of Time magazine, that she and "Bill" were "talking" (that word again) about having or adopting a new baby. We are "talking about it more now," she breathed. "I must say we're hoping to have another child." Duly reproduced—if you allow the expression—in print, the revelation pointed up the difference in child-bearing or even child-adopting age between her husband and the creaking Senator Bob Dole, later to be a talking, if not exactly walking, advertisement for the wonder-working properties of Viagra. None of the supposed "attack dogs" of the self-regarding New York press has yet asked what happened to that unborn or unconceived or unadopted child. Evidently, it took a different kind of village.

In the same way, a woman whose main claim to sympathy is the supposed violation of her intimate privacy, and that of her notorious husband, made an on-the-record incitement to journalists in 1992, telling my Vanity Fair colleague Gail Sheehy: "I don't understand why nothing's every been said about a George Bush girlfriend. I understand he has a Jennifer, too." Especially outrageous was the "too," in view of the fact that she had hysterically denied that Clinton had a "Jennifer" at all. Or perhaps it all depends on what the spelling of "Gennifer" is. (For the record, I myself investigated and ventilated the Jennifer Fitzgerald story in 1988: it seemed at least plausible that there had been an affair but not that Ms. Fitzgerald had (a.) been awarded her government job in return for sexual favors, or (b.) been denounced as either a nut or a slut by her former lover when embarrassed, or (c.) been asked to perform sexual acts while Bush was on the telephone in the Oval Office, or (d.) been overheard by a foreign embassy's electronic eavesdroppers while in the course of a phone-sex session linking the White House and the Watergate building, or (e.) been farmed out to a job in the Pentagon or the United Nations, or (f.) bitten on the mouth, or (g.) raped. If there was an affair, it was strictly consensual. And even Bushes are allowed some privacy, and can be expected to lie about sex.) Mrs. Clinton went on to help hire sordid private dicks like Terry Lenzner and Jack Palladino; a banana-republic auxiliary police for a White House who lied and lied and lied—not just about the sex, but about the women.

It's possible to feel a certain sympathy for the poor old American Right when confronted with this most protean and professional antagonist. They wish—how they wish—to convict her as the secular humanist, feminist, subversive schoolmarm they need her to be. And she goes on evading their net. Her main crimes have been the ones alleged by Jerry Brown and Ralph Nader in 1992—the transmutation of public office into private interest and vice versa, via a nexus of shady property deals and Savings and Loans. (Not a nexus that Reagan fans show any special willingness to unravel.) She is a dogged attender at church and a frequent waffler at Prayer Breakfasts and similar spectacles. She is for sexual abstinence, law and order, and the war on drugs. She stands by her man. She is for a woman's right to "choose," but then so are most Republican ladies these days. She used to be a Goldwater girl and a preachy miss, and it shows. She once assured Larry King that "there is no Left in the Clinton White House."

In 1992, the GOP's "opposition research" people thought they had her. It emerged that twenty years before, she had worked as a summer intern from Yale Law School in the deep-Red law firm of Bob Treuhaft, husband of Jessica Mitford. This firm had long handled all the radical labor cases in the Bay Area—leading Jessica or "Decca" to discover the scandal of the American funeral industry and its annexation of the death benefit, and to write the imperishable exposé *The American Way of Death*. In 1972, the same firm was heavily engaged in providing legal defense to the Black Panther Party, which for all its crimes and depredations was in physical danger from the Oakland police department.

Here was an actual and potential "gotcha." But by the time the Bush-Quayle team found it out, their private polls showed that American voters recoiled in principle from any attacks on the wife of candidate Clinton. So the material was reluctantly laid aside, to resurface every now and then in books and pamphlets written by rancorous conservatives who can't believe, even today, that Mr. and Mrs. Clinton escaped the nemesis of the law. I can scarcely believe it either but I can clear up a point or two.

Decca Mitford was a dear friend of mine; an honorable and brave ex-Communist, and a foe of all bores and all bigots. In the carrying tones of her class, she once described the experience of knowing the young Hillary Rodham.

A nice enough girl if a bit intense . . . married this young chap who later
became the governor of Arkansas. We had a client on Death Row there,
extradited from California. Turned out to be innocent, by the way, no
thanks to Jerry Brown who let him be extradited. Anyway I thought I'd
pop across to Little Rock and look up Miss Hillary. Got asked to tea on
the strength of an old acquaintance, made my pitch for the poor defendant, got a flea in my ear. Situation all changed; big political prospects
for the happy couple; not interested in reopening the case. Realism, I
think she said. The real world. Perfectly *ghastly* if you ask me.

She went on to express herself forcefully about the corporate Clintons,
and about the slimy speech that Bill had made at Nixon's funeral.

Returning from California, and from seeing the splendid Ms. Mitford
in the fall of 1994, I met Hillary Clinton one-on-one for the first and last
time. Wondering what she'd say, I brought her the greetings of Decca
and Bob. Even in a roomful of liberals—this was Sidney Blumenthal's
birthday party, on the eve of Newt Gingrich's clean midterm sweep—she
could not disown the connection fast enough. "Oh yes, I think I was there
for a very short period." She had put that behind her and moved on.

At whose expense is this irony, if it is indeed an irony at all? Partly at the
expense of the Right, which clings to its necessary myth of a diabolic liberal who will stop at nothing. Yet surely more at the expense of the liberals, especially the liberals of New York, willing to immolate themselves
once again for a woman who has proved over and over that she cares
nothing for their cherished "causes" but will risk anything, say anything,
pay any price, bear any burden, to get her family a big house and secure
herself a high-profile job. She is owed this, after all, for everything she has
suffered on our behalf. Where do we find such women? And how shall we

be worthy? Passing through its decadent phase, American liberalism enters the moment of the purely amnesiac.

On the morning of their inauguration in January 1993, the Clintons were observed standing on the steps of Blair House, official hospitality head-quarters of L'Enfant's grand and dignified federal city. "Fucking bitch," the President-elect screamed at his newly-minted First Lady. "Stupid mother-fucker," she riposted. We may never know what hideous story of "enabling" and betrayal lay behind this poisoning of their big day, but we can fix it in time as the one moment when both were totally candid in public, and both were utterly right on the facts. Those who would vote to prolong the presence of this partnership in public life are not doing so with the excuse of innocence or gullibility that might have obtained in 1992.

The figure of Mrs. Clinton was anticipated by Henry Adams in his tremendous novel *Democracy*, published as an anonymous satire on Washington corruption in 1880. Here we encounter Mrs. Lightfoot Lee, female manipulator extraordinaire:

> In her own mind, however, she frowned on the idea of seeking for men. What she wished to see, she thought, was the clash of interests, the interests of forty millions of people and a whole continent, centering at Washington: guided, restrained, controlled, or unrestrained and uncontrollable, by men of ordinary mold; the tremendous forces of government, and the machinery of society, at work. What she wanted was POWER.

The capitals were Adams's. Mrs. Lee in the end found the Senate a disappointment; in any case the condition of her making any headway was that she was a widow.

AFTERWORD

"Then, Patrick, you do feel it too? You do feel . . . something? It would be so bleak if you felt nothing. That's what scares women, you know."

"I do know, and you needn't be scared. I feel something all right."

"Promise me you'll always treat me as a person."

"I promise."

"Promises are so easily given."

"I'll fulfil this one. Let me show you."

After a shaky start he was comfortably into the swing of it, having recognised he was on familiar ground after all. Experience had brought him to see that this kind of thing was nothing more than the levying of cock-tax, was reasonable and normal, in fact, even though some other parts of experience strongly suggested that what he had shelled out so far was only a down payment.

—Kingsley Amis, *Difficulties With Girls*

"I asked him why he doesn't ask me any questions about myself, and . . .
is this just about sex, or do you have some interest in getting to know me
as a person?" The President laughed and said, according to Ms.
Lewinsky, that "he cherishes the time he had with me." She considered it
"a little bit odd" for him to speak of cherishing their time together "when
I felt like he didn't really even know me yet."

> —Judge Kenneth Starr, *Official Report of the Independent Counsel's*
> *Investigation of the President* (entry for January 21, 1996)

THE ABYSMAL FINALE of the Clinton folly was enacted, for every prac-
tical purpose, as if the President had a natural right to pass on his cock-
tax costs to the consumer. At no point were any political or constitutional
or even legal considerations permitted to "rise to the level," in the canting
phrase of the day, where they might disturb the orderly running and
management of the consensus and the stock market. Most bizarre of all
was the manner in which this priority appeared under its own name.

The United States Senate, before which the final hearing of the first
impeachment of an elected president took place, is perhaps the world's
most deliberately conservative political body. Owing in part to Article V
of the Constitution, it is impossible to amend the provision that grants
two senators to each state of the union, regardless of population. Thus—
in an arrangement aptly described by Daniel Lazare as one of "rotten
boroughs"—unpopulous white and rural states such as Montana and
Wyoming have the same representation as do vast and all-American and
ethnically diverse states like New York and California. (Lazare gives a
ratio of twelve to one between most populated and least populated state
in 1790; today the ratio would be sixty-seven to one—an imbalance about
which opinion has not yet been tested by polling.)

Moreover, the Senate is bound by arcana, procedural and historical, which are designed to limit not just public pressure but even public understanding. How often was it written, in the opening stages of the impeachment trial, that only one senator (and he the somewhat "unpredictable" veteran member from West Virginia, Robert Byrd) even comprehended the rule book. Like the Schleswig-Holstein question, or Bagehot's evocation of the British monarchy, the United States Senate is supposed to be immune from rational scrutiny and unintelligible to the ordinary gaze.

The decent conservative defense of such an institution would be, quite simply, that this evident flummery also furnishes a rampart against sudden gusts of demotic emotion. Such was certainly the intent of the Framers. So it was most fascinating, in the early weeks of the century's closing year, to witness the open collusion between constitutional obscurantism and the hucksterism of the polls; between antique ritual and shrewdly calculated advice on short-term media advantage; between, to go back to my beginning, the elitist style and the populist style. The clear winners in this cynical charade were the Clintonoid Democrats, who (as well as being hardened to switching and shifting between elitism and populism) could supply the most cobwebbed rules-monger on one hand—the aforementioned Senator Byrd—and the most sinuous arguments of the short-term general will on the other. Senator Daniel Patrick Moynihan, as so often, provided the fluid pivot and axis on which such a strategy could be made to turn, according to need, or according to the needs of New York's lumpen intellectuals.

During the Reagan era, the White House managers more than once managed to attain to the very nirvana of modern elitist populism—namely, they got a good press for getting a good press. I don't remember seeing the trick pulled again until the late decadence of the Clinton era, when journalists considered it their job to ridicule the very idea of a Senate trial, and when certain of the more savvy senators understood what was needful to attract a favorable story. (Reading *Sports Illustrated* on the floor of the Senate, with his back artfully turned to the press gallery, was the tactic successfully adopted by Democratic Senator Herbert Kohl of Wisconsin.) More distressing still was the open declaration that evidence would make, or could make, no difference. Since impeachment was not liked by the electorate, in either its actual or virtual forms, and not desired by Wall Street, and since conviction could only result in removal from office, it followed that no conviction was possible. From this reverse reasoning, the exclusion of witnesses was but a short step. As Hilaire Belloc put it: "The stocks were sold. The press was squared. The middle class was quite prepared."

I shall not forget the telephone call I received at home, on the Sunday before the final vote (February 7) from a Democratic senator not known for his political caution. He was, he said, now minded to vote for conviction on the obstruction of justice point. He also said that he felt the House of Representatives should have impeached Clinton for abuse of power: the one count that did not involve the cock-tax fallout, and that would have raised evident matters of the public interest. I was encouraged by something in his tone, and then discouraged again. "They haven't presented the case very well," he offered, as if the Republicans had really been allowed to present their case at all. "And they seem so partisan ..." As soon as the keyword of the moment had escaped his lips, I knew all I needed to know. I asked him whether it wouldn't seem "partisan" if not a single Democrat voted to convict. I suggested that, if power had been abused and justice obstructed, as he thought, it might have been nice if more people on the Left had troubled to notice it. To overlook the matter, and to leave it to the conservatives to call attention to it, and then to speak of a right-wing conspiracy, appeared to me in the light of the grossest casuistry. (There was something triangular about it.) "Anyway," I closed by saying, "now I know what you think, and you know I know, and if you end up voting with the bloc, then only I will know." And then we ended—we really did end—with mutual expressions of esteem. He did his duty by the party on the following Friday.

The words "only I will know" had by then acquired a special "resonance," as people tend to say in Washington, in my own head. On January 23, Clinton's chief defense counsel, Mr. Charles Ruff, had told the Senate in rotund terms:

> Let me be very clear about one proposition which has been a subtheme running through some of the comments of the [House] managers over the last many days. The White House, the President, the President's agents, the President's spokespersons, no one has ever trashed, threatened, maligned, or done anything else to Monica Lewinsky. *No one.* (my italics)

No knowledgeable person witnessing that statement—and there were many such witnesses—could be unaware of its complete falsity. To take one example: James Warren, the redoubtable bureau chief of the *Chicago Tribune*, commented later on CNN:

> I can tell you one thing, having listened to Mr. Ruff yesterday or the day before talk about the injustice done to the White House by reports that they were bad-mouthing her, and that they were calling her a stalker. That comment by Ruff was so palpably untrue. If I had a buck for

every person at the White House who bad-mouthed her to me last
January I could leave the set now and head off to Antigua.

This direct contradiction, on an apparently small matter, had momentous
implications. One of Mr. Ruff's deputy counsels, Ms. Cheryl Mills, had
earlier instructed the Senate that in order to prove obstruction of justice
it was necessary to show that a witness had been offered inducements *and*
subjected to threats. This is actually untrue: it is sufficient to prove that a
potential witness has been exposed to *either* sort of pressure. However,
after Clinton had involved the White House, the Pentagon, the U.S. mis-
sion to the UN, and his soft-money chief whip Vernon Jordan in trying to
find Ms. Lewinsky a job, the "inducement" business required no further
demonstration. With the spreading of allegations about stalking and
blackmail, one could hear the other shoe dropping. Lewinsky was being
warned of what might happen to her if she did not stay perjured. The
House managers in the trial had become aware of this fact, and had made
a good deal of it in the trial. There was thus a salient difference, on an
important point of evidence.

At this point, I became the hostage of a piece of information that I
possessed. Returning to Washington from the University of California,
where I had been teaching the previous spring, I had gone with my wife
for a "catch-up" lunch with our old friend Sidney Blumenthal. Filling us
in on what we had missed by being out of town when the scandal broke,
he said that what people didn't understand, and needed to know, was the
following: Monica Lewinsky had been threatening the president. Sidney
had firsthand knowledge of the truth of this story (which I later discovered he also related, along with its original Presidential authorship, to the
grand jury). Perhaps to spare my feelings or to avoid any too-obvious

insult to my intelligence or our friendship, he did not include Clinton's portrayal of himself as the prisoner Rubashov in *Darkness at Noon*. But otherwise, his account of the Chief Magistrate's sufferings was as it later appeared in the Starr Report.

At the time, I remember thinking—but not saying—that the story seemed axiomatically untrue. Even if Ms. Lewinsky had stalking and blackmailing tendencies, it remains the case that a president cannot be interrupted—except conceivably by his wife—in his "own" Oval Office. Apart from anything else, the suggestion also sat ill with Clinton's repeated claim, sometimes when under oath, that he and Ms. Lewinsky had never been alone together. Also at the time, I was more struck by the tone Sidney adopted in speaking about Kathleen Willey, whose allegations of a direct sexual lunge by Clinton had been aired on the program *60 Minutes* the previous weekend. "Her poll numbers look good now," he said rather coldly, "but you watch. They'll be down by the end of the week." As indeed they were. The White House, which when subpoenaed in the Jones case had been unable to locate them, rapidly unearthed all Ms. Willey's private notes to Clinton and made them public in one day.*

The "stalker" story had appeared extensively in print by then, immediately following the president's false claim to Sidney (a claim which he later, in his Senate testimony, truthfully described as a lie). I believe that clippings to this effect were in a folder of material that he brought along to give me, and which I no longer possess. I also believe that at least two other senior White House aides were involved in spreading the smear

---

* In April 2000, a Federal Judge found Clinton guilty of a criminal violation of the Privacy Act for this piece of squalor, which was concocted with the First Lady and Sidney Blumenthal.

against a defenseless and vulnerable young woman, who was not known at the time to possess any "forensic" evidence. One may imagine what would have been said about her, and done to her, if her garments had not once been flecked with DNA. Again at the time, the worst thing about the allegation was that Sidney seemed to believe it. It did not, for some months, acquire the significance that it assumed at trial.

In different formats and forums, including once in print, I passed the story along as an instance of what people have to believe, and how they have to think and speak, if they work for Clinton. I was readying another column on the subject when I was contacted by the chief investigative counsel of the House Judiciary Committee, on the Friday before the last day of Clinton's trial, and asked if I would put my name to it again. Had I decided not to cooperate (and on the assumption that no attempt to compel my testimony would have been made), then only I need have known. The door marked "insider" would have shut noiselessly behind me. My decision, to carry on saying what I knew to be true, was in one way very easy. Having made it plain that I would not testify against anyone but Clinton, and only in his Senate trial (an option I would have forfeited by any delaying tactics), and having understood that I had lodged this point with my interlocutors, I signed an affidavit confirming my authorship of the story, and the president's authorship of a vulgar and menacing slander. The consequences in my own life have made a literal truth out of what I had once written only metaphorically: Clintonism poisons everything it touches.

I had not known, when I met Sidney Blumenthal that day, that Kathleen Willey had already begun to experience harassment at her home, and that on the Monday after our lunch, she would receive a call from private investigator Jarrett Stern, who had sickened of his work. He warned her to be careful. It hasn't even crossed my mind, at any time since, that Sidney would have or could have had anything to do with any sleazy tactics, or even possess any knowledge of them. But I do have to say that I didn't like the tone he had acquired since we last met, and that in my memory it came to symbolize a certain *mens rea* in the Clinton White House.

There's been a certain amount made of the subject of journalistic etiquette in these matters. Suppose, then, that I had lunched with some George Bush flack in 1986, who had apologized for being late because the vice-president had been delayed by the prolixity of Oliver North. The information would have been trivial at the time. But then suppose that I saw the same George Bush raise his hand a year later, to swear that he had never even met Oliver North. I would then be in possession of evidence. And it would be too easy (as a matter of fact, it already is much too easy) for any administration to make journalists into accomplices by telling them things, often unasked for, and then holding them to the privileges of confidentiality. Had such an occasion arisen in 1986 or 1987, I would certainly have made public what I knew. (I would have told Sidney, among others.) The pact which a journalist makes is, finally, with the public. I did not move to Washington in order to keep quiet and, as a matter of fact, nobody has yet asked me to do so. Nor am I usually given inadvertent glimpses of obstruction of justice, even by the sincerest apologists.

There's a simple proof of what I mean here. The House Committee staff never asked me about Kathleen Willey. I voluntarily cited her only as part of the material of the conversation, and included the mention of her in the final affidavit because I had later come to believe that she was the victim of an injustice. Not one reporter or commentator dwelt on this for more than an instant: I suppose because it involved no conflict of evidence between Sidney Blumenthal and myself, and thus it didn't help the "story" about fratricide at Washington dinner tables. But I knew or suspected by then that Clinton would "walk," as they say, and I wanted to reproach those who had voted for his acquittal in the hope of a quick disposal of all charges about his exploitation of women and his use of the soft-money world to cover it up. They did not deserve to be able to say that they had not been told in time. (I made the same point, to no effect, in a *Washington Post* column published amid a pelting calumny on February 9, 1999.) By then, too, I knew about Juanita Broaddrick, and a few other things.

Hannah Arendt once wrote that the great success of Stalinism among the intellectuals could be attributed to one annihilating tactic. Stalinism replaced all debate about the merit of an argument, or a position, or even a person, with an inquiry about motive. I can attest, in a minor key, to the effect of this tactic in smaller matters. It was instantly said of me that I did what I did in order to promote this very book—still then uncompleted. Other allegations against me failed to rise to this elevated level. The truth or otherwise of what I had said was not disputed so much as ignored. When the finger points at the moon, the Chinese say, the idiot looks at the finger. As a much-scrutinized digit, I can attest to the effect of that, too.

The acquittal of Clinton, and the forgiving by implication of his abuses of public power and private resources, has placed future crooked presidents in a strong position. They will no longer be troubled by the independent counsel statute. They will, if they are fortunate, be able to employ "the popularity defense" that was rehearsed by Ronald Reagan and brought to a dull polish by Clinton. They will be able to resort to "the privacy defense" also, especially if they are inventive enough to include, among their abuses, the abuse of the opposite sex. And they will only be impeachable by their own congressional supporters, since criticism from across the aisle will be automatically subjected to reverse impeachment as "partisan." This is the tawdry legacy of a sub-Camelot court, where unchecked greed, thuggery, and egotism were allowed to operate just above the law, and well beneath contempt.

I composed the title of this book, and had written most of its opening passages, before I was asked to repeat under oath what I had already attested. I regret very much that the only piece of exposed flank, in a sadly successful Clintonian defense based exclusively on Clintonian lies, was offered by the confused testimony of an old friend, who was wrongly placed in the seat where the president should have sat. I had my chance to lie to the House counsel (and to lie transparently at that) or to affect amnesia, or to run out the clock and perhaps later be required to testify against an underling. I decided that in the latter case I would sooner be held in contempt, but it took no time to make up my mind that I would-n't protect Clinton's lies, or help pass them along. I wasn't going to be the last one left to lie to.

Anyway, it was a pleasure and a privilege to be hated and despised in Clinton's Washington, and also to discover that those who preached ever-lasting lenience and the gospel of the "non-judgmental" could at last summon the energy to cast a stone, even if only at myself.

A year or so later, it sometimes seemed as if the whole scandal had never been. By forcing an informal plebiscite not on his own personal and political morality, but on the morality of everybody *except* himself, Clinton had achieved the acme of corruption that comes with the enlist-ment of wide and deep complicity. Most politicians can only dream of such an outcome: Huey Long was one. By chance during that bizarre and shame-faced closure I heard a zoologist talking in Georgetown about the relationship between mammals and reptiles. "The reptile," she said, "can break into the mammal's nest and destroy and eat all the young, and be burrowed into the still-warm and living flank of the mother, before any reaction is evident. Our anthropomorphic verdict would be that reptiles don't even know that they are lucky, while mammals don't really believe that reptiles can exist."

The impression has been allowed to solidify that there was no price to be paid for all this; that the very definition of political skill was an ability to act without conscience. Appalled by the sheer raw ruthlessness of the President and his defenders, the Republicans and the conservative churches decided to call it a day. Marvin Olasky, the born-again Rightist who had originated the idea of "welfare reform" and been at Newt Gingrich's elbow, wrote a book on Presidential morality in which he said that if only Clinton had been a more regular churchgoer, and would even now ask for God's mercy, all might be well. It was not only liberals who failed the test set by Clintonism: the world of the "prayer breakfast" was his ally as surely as were the boardrooms and the Dow Jones. But millions of Americans still realized that something had been lost in the eight years of reptilian rule. The embarrassing emptiness of the 2000 election, especially the loss by the Democratic Party of even the slightest claim to any moral or ethical advantage, is one small symptom of what has been so casually thrown away. Meanwhile, the warm-blooded and the thin-blooded could only discuss the scaly and the remorseless in hushed tones, as the ensuing chapter will demonstrate. Perhaps one day the hot-blooded will have their revenge . . .